THE LION, THE WITCH AND THE WARDROBE

Table of Contents – Official Strategy Guide

Introduction

More than 50 years after they were written, C.S. Lewis's tales of good, evil, and the power of family are recognized classics. For all of those years, young and old alike have yearned to join Peter, Susan, Edmund, and Lucy on their quest to bring peace and safety to the land of Narnia.

Now, thanks to Buena Vista Games and Walden Media, this dream has become a reality. Throughout *The Chronicles of Narnia: The Lion, the Witch, and the Wardrobe*, you play as each of the four Pevensie children in their grand adventure to bring down the evil White Witch.

In this book, you will learn everything you need to know to help ensure the liberation of Narnia.

Some aspects of playing the game depend on what system you are using (PlayStation 2, Xbox, or GameCube).

Read the Manual: This introduction is only very brief. Please check the manual that came with your copy of The Chronicles of Narnia: The Lion, The Witch, and the Wardrobe for more information on basic gameplay.

The Main Screen

The main screen provides all the information you need throughout the game.

1. **Character Icon:** Indicates which of the four Pevensie children you are currently playing.
2. **Next Character / Cooperative Player:** The character being played by the second player when gaming cooperatively.

3. **Health:** Shows how much health you have remaining. When the meter runs out, the character dies.

4. **Energy Meter:** Shows how much energy the character has. Energy may be used for combination attacks (Peter and Edmund) or healing (Lucy). For Susan the meter indicates the number of arrows she has remaining.

5. **Weapon:** Which weapon the child is currently carrying.

6. **Objective Icon:** When there are time related or enemy related objectives, this icon indicates either how much time or how many enemies remain until the objective is completed.

7. **Coins:** Shows how many coins have been collected. Coins may be used to purchase abilities.

8. **Statues:** Indicates the number of statues collected so far in the current chapter. Statues may be traded in before The Great Battle in exchange for reinforcements—the more statues you have collected, the larger the number of reinforcements you can recruit.

9. **Bonus Items:** Shows how many bonus items you have collected. Bonus items unlock bonus materials that you can find in the drawer at the bottom of the wardrobe.

TIP

Pause / Start Menu: Normally you can not see the number of coins, statues, or bonus items you have collected. To check these numbers at any time, press the pause or start button.

Tumnus's Pan Pipe

In Chapter 5 (To Western Wood) Susan gets hold of Mr. Tumnus's pan pipe and almost immediately she is able to play a tune on it that makes the marauding Wolves nearby go to sleep. That's only one of the pipe's four abilities.

To see if there's a note nearby, press the ability button. Once the note has been found, Susan must step on the note, use the action button to access the "sheet music", then play the sequence of buttons shown.

Each ability is denoted by a different color note that appears on the ground:

- **Blue:** Puts nearby enemies to sleep.
- **Red:** Shatters the rocks surrounding statues.
- **Green:** Retrieves a bonus item.
- **Gold:** Calls Aslan to finish off an enemy, or allow you to progress further in a chapter.

For Susan to successfully play a note, she can not be attacked by an enemy until the entire sequence is ended.

1 The Pevensie Children

Each of the four children is unique and brings his or her own distinct style of play to the game. From straight-forward attacks, to magical tunes, to an ability to heal, the skills and talents of all four children are needed to bring an end to the White Witch's tyranny.

Peter

Being the oldest, Peter always gives orders—at least that's the way Edmund sees it. It's not so much that Peter gives orders, but that he feels responsible for his brother and sisters now that they've been sent from war torn London to the country estate of Professor Kirke.

In Narnia, Peter, as the oldest, is naturally stronger than any of the other children. He can handle a stick or a sword as a deadly weapon, which is good considering the nasty beasts they come up against.

As the game progresses and Peter gets to be more adept at using weapons, his sword (and stick) fighting abilities get stronger. He is able to gain additional attack moves, called combination attacks, that make him far more deadly.

Tip

Combination Attacks: These additional attacks require combinations of buttons to be pressed on your gamepad.

- **Bane:** The ability to kill a Wolf, Ghoul, Minoboar, Ogre, or Boggle with a single stroke. Each bane (Wolf Bane, Ghoul Bane, etc.) is acquired separately as Peter acquires greater skill with his weapons.

If several Wolves, Ghouls, Boggles, etc. are close together, he can take them out at the same time!

- **Lion's Claw:** Lion's Claw does moderate damage to all enemy creatures near Peter.
- **Lion's Leap:** Peter leaps into the air and, when he lands, slams his sword into the ground. The move does serious damage to all enemies near Peter.
- **Lion's Roar:** After Peter makes this attack, a tongue of flame runs along the ground. This attack strikes at enemies far away and must be aimed toward the monster you wish to attack.
- **Shield Slam:** One of Peter's most powerful attacks, shield slam can take out many opponents at once.

Susan

The oldest girl, Susan excels at long range attacks. Whether it's tennis balls, snowballs, or even fire arrows, Susan is the one child who is able to attack monsters that are far away. This makes her invaluable when going up against Dwarf archers, or when you need to open a window to let some nasty bats out of a room.

TIP

Fight Fire: Susan's snowballs are also able to put out fires.

This does not mean that she can't hit enemies that are up close. Though not as strong at close range as Peter or Edmund, Susan's unique pirouette punches do moderate damage.

Susan also comes into possession of Mr. Tumnus's Pan pipe. Nearly every chapter has a note inscribed somewhere on the ground that Susan can activate, then play the tune on the pipe. There are several kinds of notes: green ones that release special bonus items. Blue notes put all enemies in the area to sleep. Red ones show the locations of hidden statues, and gold ones call Aslan forth to help the children.

- **Blue:** Puts nearby enemies to sleep.
- **Red:** Shatters the rocks surrounding statues.
- **Green:** Retrieves a bonus item.
- **Gold:** Calls Aslan to finish off an enemy, or allow you to progress further in a chapter.

Edmund

Edmund is misunderstood by his siblings—he tries to gain esteem and power by tearing others down. His need for acceptance is used by the White Witch to lure his brother and sisters into Narnia. He doesn't realize that the Queen asks him this so that she may kill them and keep her reign from coming to an end.

Edmund separates himself from the rest of the children when he learns that Aslan is returning to Narnia. He did not understand the part that he and his siblings are to play in the Witch's demise…and what her plans for them are.

It is up to Peter to rescue Edmund from the clutches of the Witch's henchman, Ginarrbrik. Edmund eventually redeems himself, and comes to be a valuable addition to the team.

He also becomes skilled with sticks and swords. As he stays longer in Narnia, he also gains the combinations attacks that Peter has acquired. These two brothers make deadly enemies for any of the Witch's allies.

Tip

Combination Attacks: These additional attacks require combinations of buttons on your gamepad.

- **Bane:** The ability to kill a Wolf, Ghoul, Minoboar, Ogre, or Boggle with a single stroke.
- **Lion's Claw:** Lion's Claw does moderate damage to all enemy creatures near to Edmund.
- **Lion's Leap:** Edmund leaps into the air and, when he lands, slams his sword into the ground doing serious damage to all enemies near Edmund.
- **Lion's Roar:** A tongue of flame runs along the ground. This attack strikes at enemies far away and must be aimed toward the monster you wish to attack.

Lucy

It is Lucy that everyone has to thank for their adventures in Narnia. Were it not for her sneaking into the old wardrobe during a game of hide and seek, they might never have had the opportunity to save an entire world from the horrors of the White Witch and her winter without end.

Only a few short seconds after arriving in Narnia, her siblings (the ones who hadn't been in Narnia before) realize they were wrong in doubting her.

Though she looks young and helpless, Lucy is a tough and able fighter. Not as fast as her older siblings, Lucy's punches are strong but it is her ability to heal that makes her so valuable. It is sometimes all that keeps her family alive through their troubles.

Lucy also has an innate ability to bond with animals. It is this bond that keeps Mr. Tumnus from turning her over to the White Witch.

The bond also allows her, as she comes to know the terrible beasts of Narnia, to temporarily tame Wolves, Ghouls, Boggles, and Minoboars. Tame might actually be too nice a term to use since these horrible creatures do not sit up and beg, but instead allow Lucy to ride them. She can use them as weapons against their own kind. She has to make two to seven hits depending on the strength of the monster to get them under her control.

Aslan's Allies

Throughout their adventures, the Pevensie children meet several inhabitants of Narnia that aid them in their quests.

Aslan

Aslan is the creator of Narnia and its one, true king. A great lion, his eyes show the weight of the responsibility that he carries. He has been gone from Narnia for ages and ages because he has so many other worlds to care for.

Aslan is great and powerful. His roar can shake mountains and his singing…his singing can create worlds.

He is gentle and caring. His sacrifice leads the White Witch's to think that she is free to rule all of Narnia.

Mr. Tumnus

Mr. Tumnus, a faun, is the first Narnian that the Pevensie children meet. He discovers Lucy shortly after she steps into the enchanted world. He seems just as scared of her, as she is of him. In only a few moments, though, they become fast friends.

His decision, not to turn Lucy in, is nearly his undoing. The White Witch does not suffer disobedience lightly—she takes him prisoner, destroys his belongings, and turns him into one of her statues.

Aslan, luckily, is able to heal Mr. Tumnus while reviving all of the statues that the wicked Queen has in her castle.

Mr. and Mrs. Beaver

Kind and gentle, Mr. and Mrs. Beaver are friends of Mr. Tumnus. They live in their little beehive shaped house in the Frozen Lake created by Mr. Beaver's dam. It is a cozy home, where Mrs. Beaver can do her sewing while Mr. Beaver relaxes after working on his dam or catching fish.

They take in the children after their discovery of Mr. Tumnus's imprisonment. It is from Mr. and Mrs. Beaver that the children learn some of the history of Narnia: the White Witch, Aslan, and the prophesy about two daughters of Eve and two sons of Adam.

Mr. Beaver's skill at chewing through wood comes in extremely handy several times throughout the children's adventures.

Centaurs

Part man, part Horse, centaurs make up a large part of Aslan's army. Fast runners, their hooves are deadly weapons, but centaurs are particularly dangerous because of their excellent archery skills.

Centaurs fight in two of the chapters in *The Chronicles of Narnia: The Lion, the Witch, and the Wardrobe*, the Battle of Beruna where they kill giants and the Great Battle where they act as reinforcements. They also serve as the camp guards that Susan and Lucy must evade during the chapter Follow Aslan.

Oreius

Leader of the centaurs, Oreius is the best of the best. When nearing the final showdown against the Queen's forces, it is Oreius who does battle with Otmin, her strongest Minotaur, during the Battle of Beruna.

Eagles

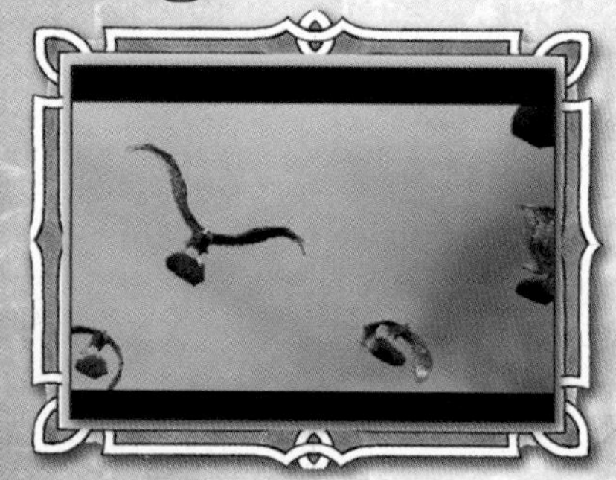

Eagles are the aerial assault arm of Aslan's army. Their method of attack is to carry large stones and drop them on the enemy. Though they only fight in two chapters of the game, their contributions are invaluable. They kill giants during the Battle of Beruna, and provide reinforcements during the Great Battle.

Father Christmas

The arrival of Father Christmas shortly after the children's adventures on the frozen lake shows just how much the White Witch's hold over Narnia is waning. Her magic had held the land in a state of winter for nearly 100 years…a winter in which it was never Christmas.

Of course Father Christmas does not come empty handed and brings the three children he meets presents. He presents Peter with a sword and shield, Susan gets a bow and arrow and an ivory horn, and Lucy receives a vial of fire-flower cordial which is medicine so strong that only one drop cures any injury. As he says, these gifts are not toys, but are tools to aid to the children as they battle against the forces of evil in the land.

The White Witch's Forces

During the children's adventures in Narnia they come up against a host of adversaries intent on killing them. Knowing the creatures and how to defeat them is paramount if Narnia is to emerge as a free land once more.

Bosses

Queen Jadis, the White Witch

The ultimate evil, Queen Jadis, also known as the White Witch, has usurped Aslan's rightful throne. Armed with her powerful magic, she is able to turn any creature into a statue, frozen for all time. It is also her magic that has brought perpetual winter to Narnia for over 100 years.

She is encountered in battle only during the final chapter, appropriately titled *The White Witch*.

General Otmin

The Witch's most powerful Minotaur, Otmin is extremely difficult to kill. He is the final enemy to be defeated in the Battle of Beruna, after you have already fought giants, Minoboars, Ogres and a whole host of other vile creatures.

Ginarrbrik

The Queen's most trusted servant, Ginarrbrik is tough as nails and as mean as they come. His one weakness is when he gets dizzy. Until he is vulnerable, it is best to keep your distance from the Dwarf.

Maugrim

Leader of the Wolves and the White Witch's Chief of the Secret Police, Maugrim is a tenacious enemy who pursues the children all the way to Aslan's Camp.

Soldiers

Ankle Slicers

Small, pale, and fast, Ankle Slicers may seem just a nuisance, but they can be a danger when encountered in great numbers. Their speed makes them difficult to hit, since they can zip right around the children. The best attack against them is to have Peter or Edmund hit them with sticks or swords. Usually one hit is enough to kill the little creatures.

Boggles

Slow and stupid, Boggles are nonetheless a tough opponent. Generally traveling in packs, it is best to attack these beasts with Peter's or Edmund's sticks and swords. When available, their Boggle Bane combination attack can take out one or more boggles at a time, making it invaluable for dealing with the packs of marauders.

Black Dwarfs

Black Dwarfs are the enemy army's archers. Able to attack the children from far away, they are crack shots and can pose a great danger. Susan, armed with snowballs and, later, her bow and arrows, is the child best suited to dealing with this menace.

Cyclopes

Cyclopes are one of the toughest opponents you come across. Typically they are invulnerable to simple sword, stick, and only slightly vulnerable to the boys' combination attacks. When up against Cyclopes, killing them quickly requires hitting them with bundles of flaming sticks. Each burning bundle deals 50% damage to single eyed monstrosities (25% in Hard mode).

TIP

Boggle Tame: Lucy can tame Boggles, riding them and using her new mount to attack the enemy.

Ghouls

Quick and lithe, Ghouls usually attack in large numbers. When far away, Susan's arrows do heavy damage against these creatures, but her pirouette attacks do little damage when they are close. It is best to attack Ghouls with swords and sticks. Peter and Edmund can, eventually, gain the Ghoul bane combination attack which allows them to kill one or more Ghouls with a single blow.

TIP

Ghoul Tame: Lucy can tame Ghouls, using them to attack its allies.

Horrors

Dark, mysterious, and impervious to any attack, Horrors inhabit the White Witch's castle, feasting on many of the statues she has imprisoned there. To drive them off the statues, Susan and Lucy must bring light into the chambers they occupy. Once they have been "enlightened" they fly around the area menacing the girls. Though they do little damage, the sheer number of them can cause problems. The best defense against Horrors is to stay away from them until they eventually dissipate. Do not come close to a Horror while it is still feasting on a statue or it can cause serious damage.

Minoboars

Minoboars can inflict serious damage when encountered in packs. They are relatively easy to kill with a sword or stick and, when it becomes available, the boys' Minoboar bane combination attack can kill one or more with a single blow.

Minotaur

Larger than Minoboars, Minotaurs have the head of a bull. Far more deadly than their smaller cousins, they are also tougher to kill. Their armor and ability to parry sword and stick attacks can make it difficult to do much damage. To kill them quickly requires that the boys use combination attacks such as shield slam, lion's roar, lion's leap, or lion's claw. Their armor must be destroyed before they take damage and this can only be done with swords.

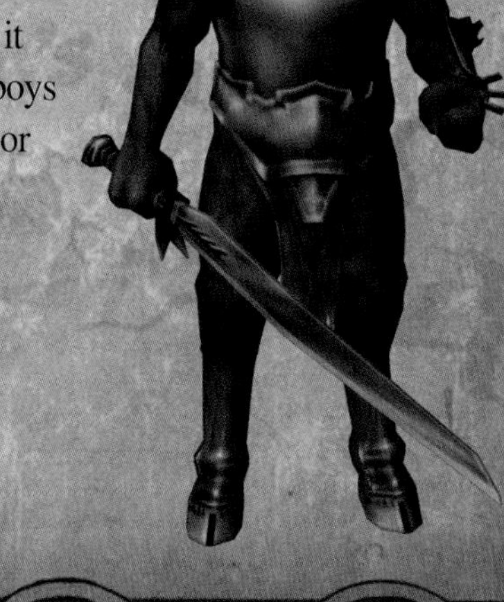

TIP

Minoboar Tame: Lucy can tame Minoboars, riding them and using them to attack the enemy.

Ogres

Tall and deadly, Ogres are tough to kill when first encountered. This is because the children have not yet become trained in their weapons and are not skilled in combination attacks. The first few times an Ogre is encountered, the children must hide. When they finally can attack, they must all work together to defeat a single Ogre. Finally, though, the boys become adept at the Ogre bane combination attack which can take out these massive beasts in a single shot.

Wolves

One of the most common enemies encountered in Narnia, Wolves are relatively easy to kill—Susan can kill a Wolf with a single arrow and the boys can kill them with two swipes of their swords or a single Wolf Bane combination attack. The main threat from Wolves is their speed and their tendency to attack in packs.

Werebats

Werebats are the White Witch's air force. They patrol the skies carrying large rocks that they drop on the Pevensie children. Even a near miss with the rocks can cause damage and knock the children off their feet. Since they fly so high, the Werebats can not be attacked, even by Susan's arrows. The only defense against their stones is to move toward them, then continue past as they drop their payload.

Werewolves

Stronger, faster, and doing more damage than either other type of Wolf, Werewolves also have a piercing howl that can knock the children off their feet and do terrible damage. When they are about to howl the beasts stand up on their hind legs—this is a hint to run…quickly…to get out of range of their blast. Werewolves are susceptible to Susan's arrows. Even close up, her pirouette attacks do serious damage, but at that close range the ability to flee their howl is greatly diminished.

TIP

Wolf Tame: Lucy can tame Wolves, riding them to attack other creatures.

The Air Raid

World War II has come to London. The four Pevensie children are in their home when the German air force launches an air raid. You must find all the children and get them out safely.

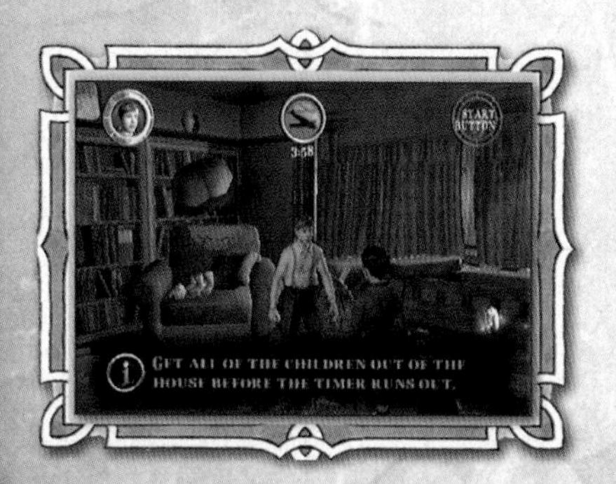

Bonus Items

Bonus items in this room can be found in the china cabinet, piano, couch, chair to the left of the fireplace, and in the mantle clock. There is also a bonus item in the mirror above the fireplace but you can't get it at the beginning.

The Bombing Begins

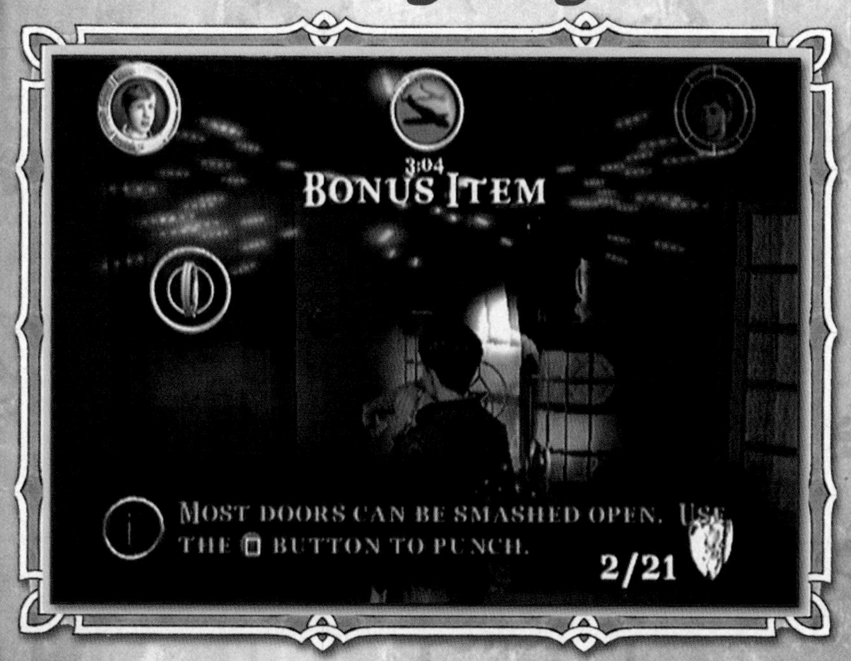

Peter and Edmund are in the drawing room. Search the room for coins and bonus items. The bombs have jammed all the doors in the house, so you have to beat them down. Peter is better at this, as he is stronger. Take control of Peter, then move to the door and hit it repeatedly.

When it breaks in, move into the front hall and speak to the children's mother. She asks you to find Lucy and Susan and get them to safety.

Find Susan

BONUS ITEMS

There is a bonus item in the corner cabinet, just outside the kitchen door. There is another that can only be found by Susan and her torch, so ignore it for now.

There are also bonus items located in two of the pictures at the top of the stairs.

Head down the hallway, gathering coins from the four cabinets. Then head up the stairs. The first two doors are totally jammed and can't be opened, so continue along the upstairs hall to the boys' room on the left.

Knock down the door and move across the room to Susan. She becomes the selected character for now.

Bonus Items

The boy's room has four bonus items: the mirror above her dressing table, the picture over the right-hand bed, and the two beds. Susan can find the bonuses in the picture and mirror, but Peter is faster at finding them in the beds.

Bonus Items

To find bonuses with Susan's torch, move so that you can see the picture or mirror and use the target button. Turn her around until the light shines on the bonus. A progress circle appears. Keep the light aimed on the bonus to fill the circle and gain the bonus.

Collect all the coins and bonuses in the boy's room, then move out to the hall.

Find Lucy

Bonus Items

Get the two bonus pictures at the top of the stairs before heading into the girls' room. The only bonus in the girls' room is located in the picture next to Lucy's bed. Susan can use her torch to find coins and this bonus while she is looking for Lucy.

When everyone is in the hallway, Peter must break down the door to the girls' room, then Susan must use her torch to see in the room.

Enter Lucy's room and turn to the left. Use the torch and sweep the room to locate the coins, bonus item, and finally Lucy who is cowering in her bed. Hit all the beds and dressers in the room to gather the coins.

Get Downstairs

Leave Lucy's room. As soon as you enter the hall, a bomb explodes and damages the floor. Although Susan tells Lucy to find a way across, Edmund should go over to the damaged area. He is stronger and can topple the grandfather clock easier.

The grandfather clock can be used as a bridge. Hit it until it is knocked over. The other children can now scamper across in safety.

Tip

Ability: With the coins you've collected, you can now purchase the double damage ability for Peter. Buy the ability or Peter can't open the next series of doors.

Bonus Items

There are three bonus items in the bedroom. One is in the cabinet, just inside the door. The second is in the picture to the right of the door. The third is in the remains of the bed.

The way down the stairs is blocked by rubble. Peter must knock down the door to the bedroom. Enter the room.

Move to the left and grab the 30 second timer to add 30 seconds to the countdown timer. Move away from the door and to the bedpost in the middle of the room.

Press the action button to get on the bedpost. Climb up it to knock it off balance. When the bedpost falls, it moves a pile of debris making a bridge for the others to cross.

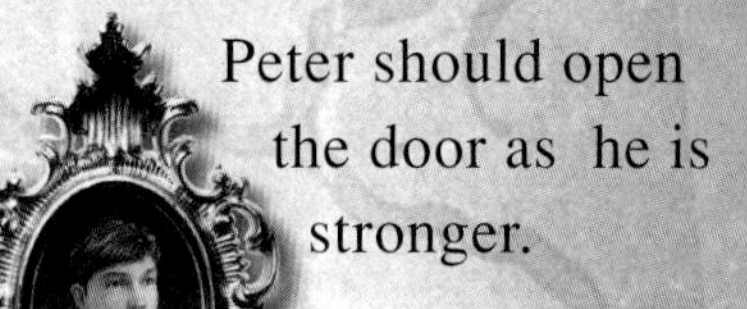

Peter should open the door as he is stronger.

Move through the broken wall into the bathroom, picking up coins along the way. Have Peter knock down the door into the hallway, leave the bathroom, and head down the stairs.

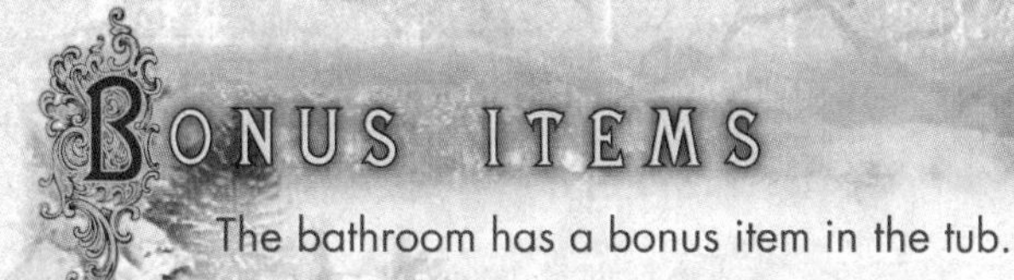

The bathroom has a bonus item in the tub.

Get to the Kitchen

The way to the kitchen is blocked. Two fires are burning up from the basement. These fires can be extinguished using the cabinets in the downstairs hall. When the first fire is out, it is a good time to send Susan into the drawing room to gather the bonus item in the mirror above the fireplace.

BONUS ITEMS

There is a bonus item in the picture across the hall from the stairs. There is another in the mirror above the fireplace in the drawing room. Susan can find each of these with her torch.

Move the second cabinet in the same way to extinguish the second fire and gain access to the kitchen.

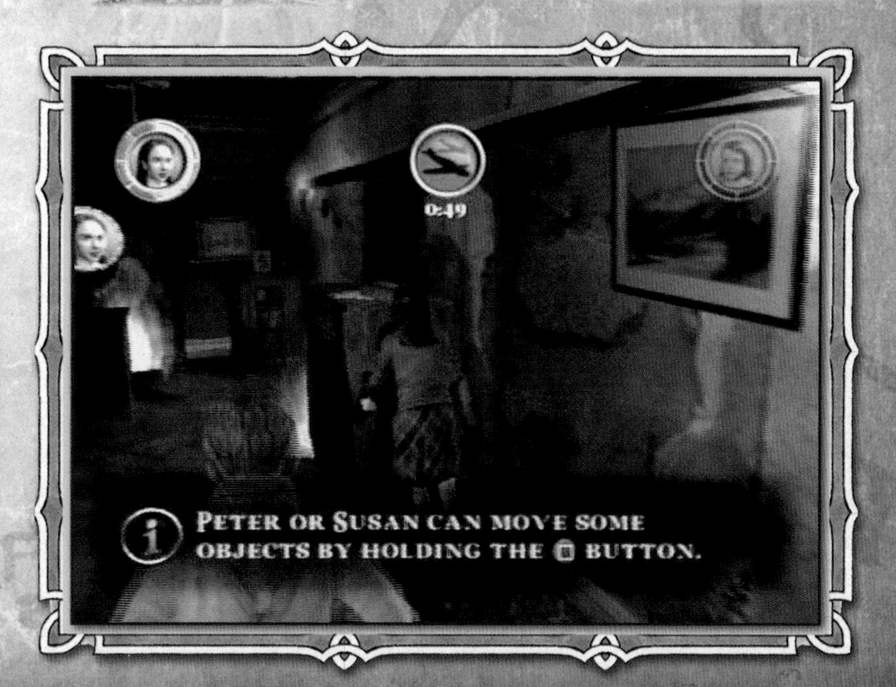

Bonus Items

The kitchen contains two Bonus Items: one in the table to the right of the outside door, and the other in one of the chairs. Peter can gather these fastest.

All of the children file into the kitchen, but escape is not as easy as opening the door to leave. It's locked!

Gather the bonus items. Susan must sweep the kitchen to the right of the exit door. There is a key in the bread box.

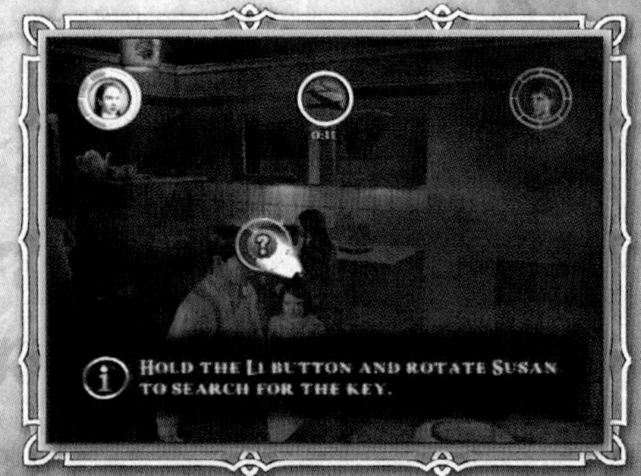

Glimpse of Narnia

While playing hide and seek, Lucy passes through the wardrobe into Narnia where she meets Mr. Tumnus. As she's heading back to the wardrobe, Lucy meets up with Edmund, who's just finished a conversation with someone he calls "your majesty". Now they must find their way back to the wardrobe...

Team Up

Bonus Items

There are two bonus items in this area. One is located under a pile of stones—have Edmund roll the bundle of sticks into the left-hand pile to gain the bonus. The other is located floating off the ground—have Lucy climb onto the snowball to get high enough to grab it.

Edmund and Lucy find themselves in a small clearing with no ready exit, so they have to make one for themselves. To the right is an ice barrier that, when you get close, says it can be knocked down once each of the team-up tokens have been collected.

One of the team-up tokens is located high off the ground. To reach this one, move Lucy up to the large snowball, then have her move forward again—she jumps up onto the snowball making her tall enough to grab the token.

Another token is located at the top of the dead tree near the ice wall. Climb the tree with Edmund to gain the token.

Next to this tree is a bundle of sticks. Directly in front of the bundle is a pile of rocks concealing the third token. Aim the sticks at the pile, then press the attack button to send the sticks toward the pile. Knock over the stones and gain the token.

The remaining tokens require a bit more firepower. Have Edmund pick up the stick that's floating to the left of the fire—this lets him gather the remaining tokens, and also provides a weapon for the battles to come.

TIP

Burning Bushes: Burning things come in handy throughout the cold Narnian missions. Whenever you have a stick, it's a good idea to light it at a fire whenever possible.

Move Edmund to the fire. The end of his stick catches fire. Take the burning stick over to the bushes located down from the fire. When the bushes catch fire, the token is released.

The final two tokens are located at the top of the clearing behind two sets of protective brambles. Move Edmund to each pile, then attack with his stick. The brambles fall away exposing the other tokens.

To the Lamppost

Once all items are collected, move the two children together. When they are highlighted, press the team up button.

Move the children toward the ice wall. When the children are close, press the attack button. Lucy slides toward the wall with such force that it shatters.

Tip

Edmund and His Stick: It is important to immediately switch to Edmund as a number of Wolves come out of the forest to attack. Edmund and his stick are far more effective against the Wolves than the unarmed Lucy.

Bonus Items

The one bonus item in this area is again located up high. Lucy has to return to the snowball and ride it back to retrieve the bonus.

Take out all the Wolves to secure the area. Lucy is then safe to retrieve the bonus token in this area.

Bonus Items

There is a bonus item at the top of the lamppost that Edmund can reach. The ravens that fly by can knock him off the post, but they won't hurt him.

Travel through the tunnel. At its end is the lamppost. Collect all the coins and health hearts here before moving on.

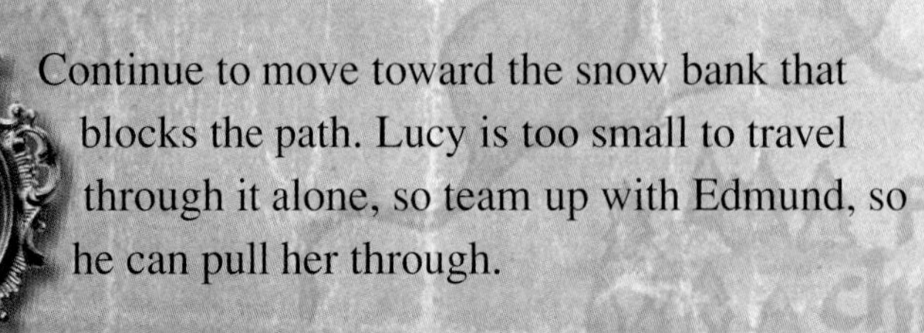

Continue to move toward the snow bank that blocks the path. Lucy is too small to travel through it alone, so team up with Edmund, so he can pull her through.

The Wolves and the Wardrobe

Tip

No Retreat: Once you get past the snow bank you can't return to the lamppost or beyond.

Bonus Items

The final bonus item is released when all of the bushes that the Wolves come through are set on fire.

Edmund's stick has probably gone out by now, so relight it at the fire just beyond the snow bank. Continue to the brambles blocking the path. Have Edmund break them, then keep following the path.

At the turn in the path, Wolves attack you. No matter how many you defeat, they keep coming. The only way to stop them is to set the three bushes where they come from on fire.

Once the threat from the Wolves is finished, keep going on the path. Have Edmund destroy the final bramble blocking the path, then continue on toward the wardrobe...

The Spare Room

Although Edmund knows the truth about Narnia, he lies just to make Lucy feel miserable. Now, Peter and Susan must find their two younger siblings and get back to their rooms to keep from making Mrs. Macready angry. She is on the lookout, so beware. If she catches you, she sends the children to their rooms.

Follow Lucy

After Lucy's tantrum, she storms out of the spare room. Follow her out the door, then head down the small stairway toward the main hallway. Enter the girls' bedroom and collect all of the coins.

Bonus Items

A bonus item is located in the table next to the bed.

Lucy is hiding under the table near the window. Have either Peter or Susan drag it out of the way. When the table is clear, Lucy bolts up and runs away again.

Follow her through the door and into the small hallway. There are crates here blocking your way and the door is locked leading back through the bedroom. You need to break the boxes to keep going.

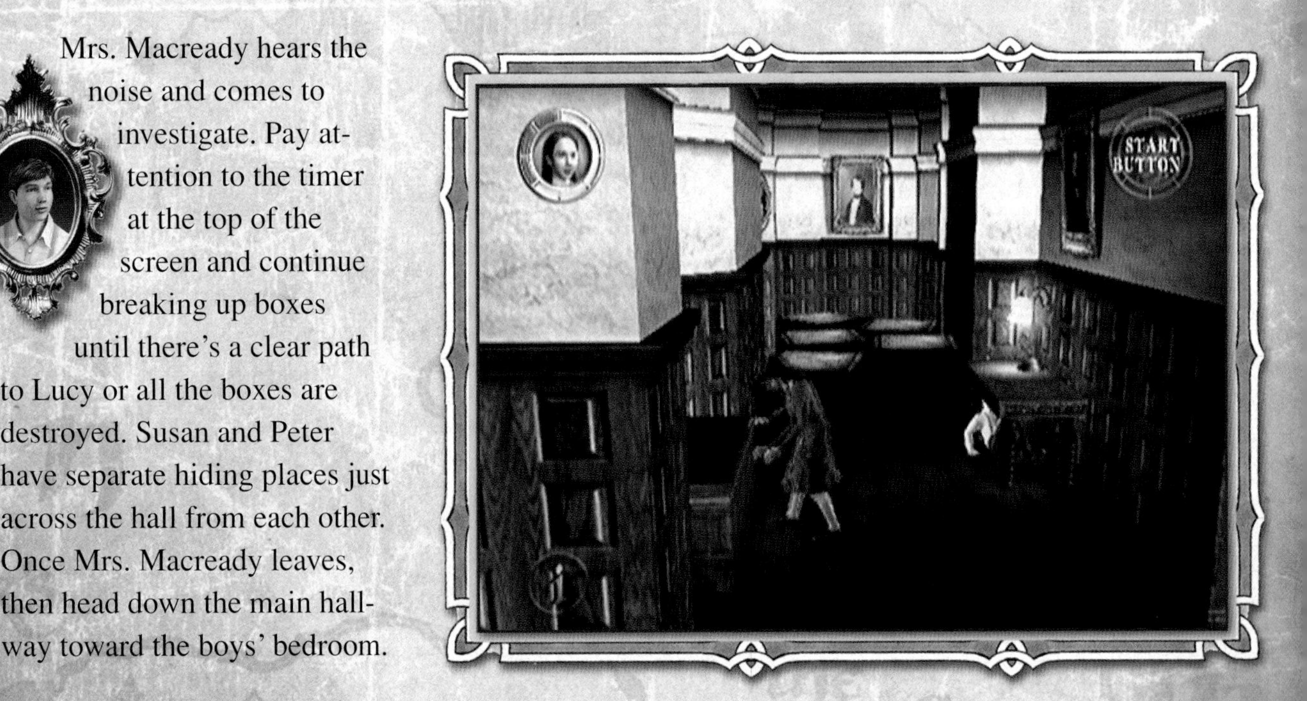

Mrs. Macready hears the noise and comes to investigate. Pay attention to the timer at the top of the screen and continue breaking up boxes until there's a clear path to Lucy or all the boxes are destroyed. Susan and Peter have separate hiding places just across the hall from each other. Once Mrs. Macready leaves, then head down the main hallway toward the boys' bedroom.

Bonus Items

There is a bonus item located in the suit of armor about halfway down the main hallway. It can be tough to see because it's hidden in an alcove.

Another bonus item is hidden in the chair in the boys' bedroom.

Once in the bedroom, pick up the tennis balls sitting on the floor between the beds—Susan needs these in a moment. Have Peter hit the candlestick near the window to knock it out of the way and reveal a secret passageway—unfortunately this also releases a swarm of bats!

Susan must throw a tennis ball at the small part of the window located on either side of the room. When she hits the window, it opens and the bats fly out.

Bonus Items

Tennis Balls: Susan can carry up to 50 tennis balls. Since the pile keeps replenishing, return to get the full 50 tennis balls before continuing on.

Secret Passage to the Drawing Room

Lucy now joins your troop. Send the children through the secret doorway.

Bonus Items

There is a bonus item halfway down the secret passage. It is hidden in an alcove, so you won't be able to see it.

Bonus Items

The two bonus items in this room are hidden behind the heating grates near the ceiling. Susan can close these grates and get the bonus items by throwing tennis balls at them. You want to close these grates anyway since they let the bats into the room.

The bats in the drawing room attack the children. Have Susan throw tennis balls at them. You can rotate her around while she is ready to throw. When a bat lights up, let the tennis ball fly.

The Entrance Hall

Bonus Items

Three bonus items are located in the great hall. One is in the chair just to the left of the stairs. Another is in the suit of armor just up the stairs on the landing. The third is located in the small room to the upper left of the suit of armor.

With the bats out of the way, continue on into the great hall.

Once you have all the coins, punch the large grate on the right-hand wall. This falls away and Lucy can fit through. Send her through; a moment later she appears at the dining room door.

The Dining Room

Bonus Items

The two heating grates in the dining room contain bonus items. Again, have Susan throw tennis balls at them to close them, sealing out the bats and gaining the bonuses.

Enter the dining room. Behind the table (located between the fireplace and suit of armor) is a stick. Have Peter or Susan pull out the table and retrieve the stick—it comes in handy breaking up boxes in a moment.

The Sitting Room and Courtyard

When the dining room is cleared out, head into the sitting room.

Bonus Items

The sitting room has two bonus items. One is in the chest next to the door and the other in the chair next to the couch.

Clear out the coins in the furniture before having Peter break through the grate under the window next to the door. When it pops open, switch to Lucy and send her through the opening. She'll appear in a moment through the doors to the courtyard.

The courtyard is full of boxes. You have to clear these away before you can get to the other side. Peter must use his stick to break his way through the crates. He should have plenty of time to break all the boxes before Mrs. Macready arrives.

Head back into the sitting room to hide. Peter's hiding spot is to the left of the door, Lucy's is just to the right of the door, and Susan's is behind the curtains.

After Mrs. Macready has checked out the sitting room, switch to Susan and return to the courtyard. Here, have her throw tennis balls through the three grates to seal out more bats and claim the bonus items.

At the far end of the courtyard, Edmund is hiding in the drain. When any of the group gets close, Peter talks him into coming out.

Bonus Items

The courtyard has three bonus items. Each of these is a grate set high on the wall. Susan needs to close these grates with her tennis balls to retrieve the bonuses.

Escape to the Children's Rooms

Have Edmund climb the drainpipe to the left of the other door. After a moment he reappears, opening the door.

Break up the boxes lining the winding staircase leading up to the small hall. Make sure to grab the 30 second extension that's in these boxes!

Every previous location is either locked or blocked by the Professor. The only place left is the spare room. Maybe the children can hide in the wardrobe...

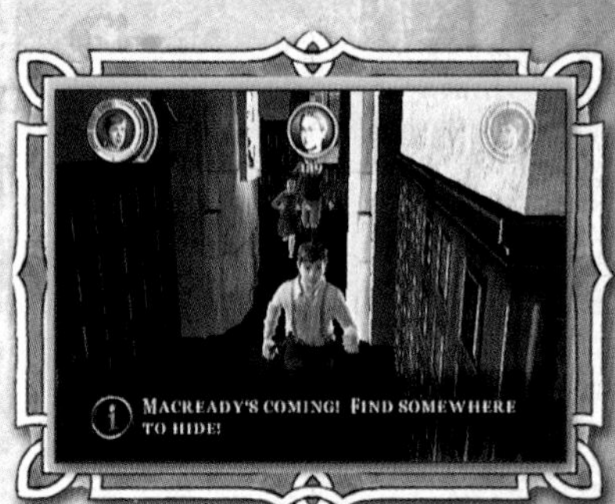

7 Lantern Waste

All of the children are now in Narnia—there's no question of believing Lucy now! When the question of what to do now comes up, Lucy suggests a visit to Mr. Tumnus.

To the Lamppost

To leave this area and get to the lamppost, Peter must break the two barrels just down from where you enter Narnia. Pick up the stick that one of these barrels holds and use it to smash through the icy brambles blocking your way. After the first brambles, you need to fight off some Wolves.

When you have broken down the second set of brambles, Lucy must jump onto the snowball from the beginning of the level. Ride it all the way to the lamppost, then have her collect all of the floating coins in the area. When you have all the floating coins, have her jump off the snowball, duck into the two small caves, and collect the coins on the ledges.

Have Susan throw snowballs at the three barrels in this area to break them without worrying about getting hurt if they explode. Exploding barrels have a green mark on them. This reveals a stick for Edmond to use.

Now that Edmund has a stick, he can climb the lamppost and light his stick—this acts as a torch when you go through the tunnel. Watch out for the ravens—they knock Edmund off the lamppost, but do not do him any harm. The easiest way to get up there is to let the ravens to pass, then immediately climb the lamppost.

Across the Chasm

When you have collected everything in the lamppost area, it's time to move on. A wall of ice blocks the entrance to the tunnel. Team up Edmund and Lucy to knock down the ice.

Once through the tunnel, collect all of the coins.

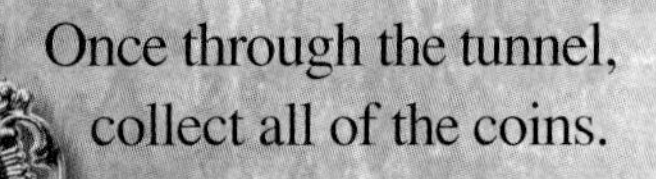

Setting fire to the bushes next to the tall stone pillar causes the barrels at the base of the pillar to explode, weakening the pillar. As soon as the bushes are on fire, team up Peter and Edmund. When the barrels explode, the pillar topples over and releases Wolves.

Now it's time for Peter to defend the group. Move him to the base of the pillar to await the onslaught of 15 Wolves that use the newly created bridge to attack the children.

When the last Wolf is beaten, the pillar finishes toppling down and is low enough for the children to climb onto and cross the chasm.

TIP

Wolf Bane: During the fight against the Wolves a new ability may become available: Wolf Bane. Purchase this ability for Peter and Edmund so that they can defeat Wolves with one hit. If you are short on coins, you may want to save your money for other abilities.

Avalanche

No sooner do the children get to the other side of the chasm than the snow and ice give way...Avalanche!

Ride the ice "sleds" down the mountain to avoid the avalanche. The only real menace on the way down is the chasms. Maneuver between the chasms to the bottom of the mountain.

Bonus Items

Twenty of the twenty-one bonus items in this chapter are in the ice piles during the avalanche. Break through the piles to collect the bonuses.

Across the Frozen Pond

Safe...for the moment. To continue on, the children must get across the first pond. The ice isn't thick enough for Peter or Susan, so one of the others has to find a safe route.

Lucy or Edmund must move out onto the ice. If the ice holds the older children, it turns blue. If not, it begins to buckle—get off that piece right away before the child you're playing falls in!

Continue searching out the path until a continuous line of blue ice runs from one side of the pond to the other. When you have found all the blue sections, the rest of the children cross the frozen pond.

Across the Running Stream

On the other side of the pond, Peter must break through the brambles and defeat the two Wolves. Once the immediate threat is gone, a new problem surfaces: how to get across the stream!

Lucy must move the snowball away from the mouth of the cave and collect the floating coins. Jump off the snowball and go into the cave. This unlocks her first aid ability. Have her collect the coins and hit the statue to collect it. Finally, move her to the bundle of sticks and push it into the river.

Move Edmund forward onto the bundle and have him ride it across to the other side of the stream. Once there, attack the tree near the water—it falls over, making a bridge for the other children.

Bonus Items

Edmund must climb the dead tree to retrieve the bonus item in its branches

Through the Frozen Gate

This portion of the chapter requires teamwork between Edmund or Peter and Susan. Edmund and Peter are the best at fighting off the Wolves that are to come, while Susan is required to throw snowballs at the Dwarf archers and also put out the flames on the gate.

Peter must break through the brambles blocking your path, then proceed down to the frozen gate. Here, have Peter knock down the three ice pieces covering the gate. Once this is done, some Dwarfs light fires on the gate to ward off the children.

Tip

Each of the ice blocks on the tree can be knocked off in one hit if Lucy teams up with a sibling and is thrown into the trees.

Susan must throw snowballs at both the fires on the gate and also the archers firing at the children. This is where the fast switching comes in—while Susan is dousing the flames and taking care of the archers, several Wolves attack. Peter and Edmund are the best at fighting off the Wolves, so use to either of them when the Wolves menace the children.

As soon as Susan has put out the fires, Peter must knock down the gate and immediately move to the other side—this stops the Wolf attacks, though you still have to worry about the archers.

Defeat the three fleeing archers. When the way in front is relatively clear, move the children forward, out of range of the archers on the left. Collect the four statues in this area. Use Susan to destroy the barrels, allowing Lucy to collect the coins in the caves.

Across the Second Pond

Move the children forward toward the second pond. Two more archers are waiting here, so have Susan throw snowballs at them to remove this threat. Use snowballs to collect the statue on the far-left ledge.

Again, this pond is not stable, Lucy must work out a path across the ice. This time it's a little tougher because a flock of ravens tries to knock her into the frozen water. Carefully cross the ice to the other side.

Through the Valley

The upcoming valley is full of archers. There is a statue to be collected to the right of the brambles. After having Peter take care of the frozen brambles, move forward and defeat the archers. Be sure to collect the three statues along the path.

TIP

Barrels: Many of the barrels in the valley are full of explosives. Susan can set them off with only a single snowball, defeating the archers that are using them for cover.

At the end of the valley is Mr. Tumnus's house—but before you can enter it, you must fight off 20 Wolves. Peter must fight off the Wolves. When the Wolves are gone, the children can proceed.

To Western Wood

When the children are finished investigating Mr. Tumnus's house, a Beaver calls them outside. Mr. Beaver, as a matter of fact. He begins to explain what has happened, but realizes that they are only safe in his house, so he leads the way.

The Pan Pipe

Mr. Tumnus's furniture has been used to create burning, makeshift barricades to block your path. Have Susan throw snowballs at the flames until they go out. Once the flames have died out any of the older children can knock down the furniture and clear the way. Make sure to collect the three statues at the beginning of the level.

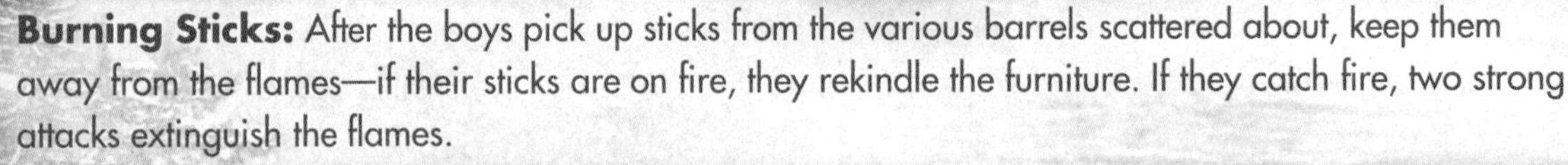

Tip

Burning Sticks: After the boys pick up sticks from the various barrels scattered about, keep them away from the flames—if their sticks are on fire, they rekindle the furniture. If they catch fire, two strong attacks extinguish the flames.

As the children pass through, Susan picks up a Pan pipe—with this she can play melodies to temporarily lull enemies to sleep (blue note), gain bonus items (green note), or reveal hidden statues (red note). To play the pipe, Susan must use her ability button to see if there is a note nearby. If there are any notes, then stand in the area indicated and "play" the keys indicated. If she is knocked off the note while playing, she must start all over again.

In the next area, burning furniture again blocks you. This time, though, there are Wolves menacing the group while you try to destroy the blockade. Have the boys keep the Wolves at bay (but don't kill them) while Susan uses her Pan pipe to play the blue note—this puts the Wolves to sleep and no more come to attack. Susan can now clear away the furniture at a more leisurely pace. Collect the two statues in this area before continuing.

Two Grey Wolves protect the next area. Dispatch them after breaking down the barrier and you can clear out this area unmolested. There are four statues here; two to the right, one on the left and one that requires Susan's Stone Song (red music note). (You will have to come back after you acquire Stone Song.)

Mr. Beaver Clears the Way

After clearing away the third batch of furniture, you are confronted by a never-ending supply of Wolves. To keep them at bay, light the bushes on both sides of the clearing on fire—as the winds of the storm pick up, these bushes and the fire at the entrance blow out letting more Wolves in. Make sure to return to rekindle the fires. You can shield yourself from the winds by standing behind the large rock. You can light your sticks at the protected fire just inside this area. There are two more statues in this area.

Bonus Items

There are 25 bonus items that are released each time you light the bushes in this area. Each time the wind blows out the fire on the bushes, relight them to gain the bonus items and help keep Mr. Beaver safe. If Mr. Beaver is too quick, though, you might not be able to get all the bonus items.

When Mr. Beaver finishes eating through the fallen trees you can continue on.

The Draw Bridge

Just past this barricade are several archers on the right side of the pass. You have to move further into this area to escape attacks by Wolves, so you are more vulnerable to attack by the archers. Have Susan pick up the bow and arrows in this area, then use it to take out the archers.

Continue on to the drawbridge. The mechanism for extending the bridge is blocked by ice. Team up Susan and Lucy to have them bash the ice away—this may take several tries. In addition to extending the bridge, it also opens a small door that Lucy can go through to gain coins.

Bonus Items

Use Lucy to enter the small door and collect the bonus item down below.

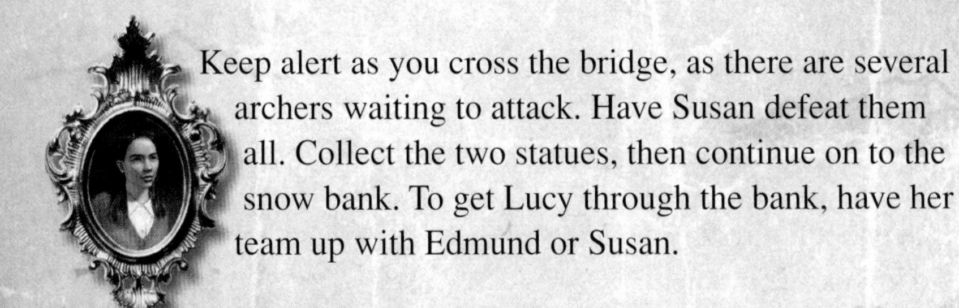

Tip

Arrows: Have Susan collect all the arrows she can from just before the bridge. She can hold 50, so return to the arrow location and pick them up until her quiver is full.

Keep alert as you cross the bridge, as there are several archers waiting to attack. Have Susan defeat them all. Collect the two statues, then continue on to the snow bank. To get Lucy through the bank, have her team up with Edmund or Susan.

On the far side is an Ogre that you cannot possibly defeat. Instead, have Susan use her Pan pipe—locate the blue note and put the Ogre to sleep.

Bonus Items

Lucy or Edmund are the only children who can pick up the two bonus items, on either side of the Ogre, as they won't *immediately* fall through the ice. When getting the items, make sure to go around the Ogre on the side you're coming *from*, as you can't return once you've reached dry land again.

The Wolf Dens

The next area is home to four Wolf dens. Each of these must be sealed off before you can proceed. There is only one statue here. It can only be collected with Susan's Stone Song (red music note) ability.

Lucy: Lucy must enter the cave and follow it to the upper level. There she needs to hit the wooden supports to collapse the upper cave area.

Susan: Have Susan shoot the rocks above her cave entrance to knock them down.

Edmund or Peter: Lighting the bushes in front of the cave keeps the Wolves at bay.

Edmund and Peter: The two boys need to team up and attack the pillar outside the final cave to cover its entrance.

When the last cave is sealed, a timer begins. This timer indicates when the Ogre arrives. Hide the children behind the rocks at the exit, before he comes through.

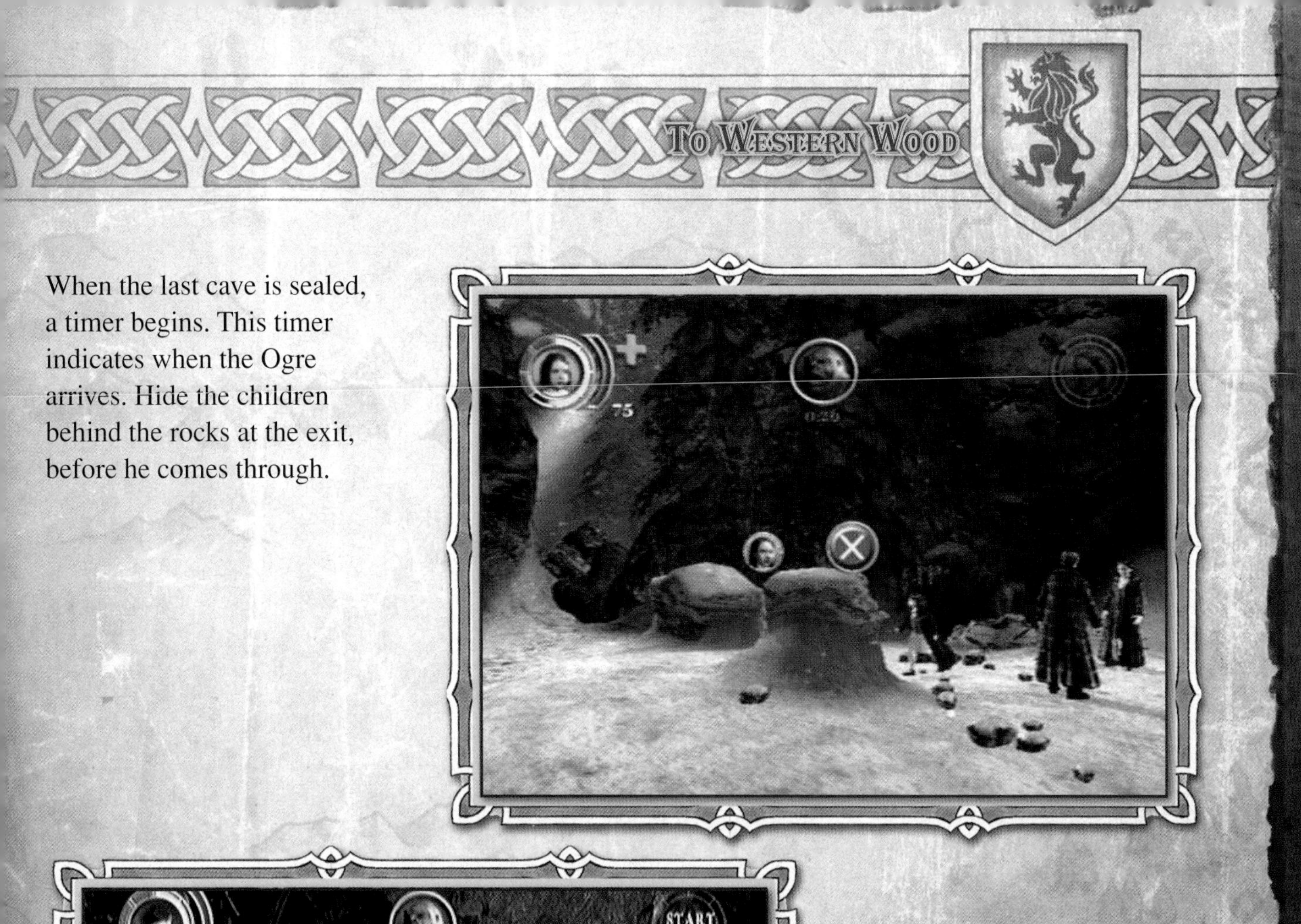

Bonus Items

There is a green note in the middle of this area. Have Susan use her Pan pipe to play the song indicated to gain the bonus. You have to return to this level after acquiring Susan's Dryad's Melody.

The Ghoul Forest

After the Ogre passes through and blasts away the rocks blocking the exit, leave the area. To the left is a dark path through the forest—follow the path, but beware of the Ghouls that drop from the trees. Have Peter defeat them quickly, because the Ogre returns.

After several of the Ghouls have been defeated, a countdown timer begins. When all the Ghouls are dead, four hiding places appear at the end of the path—get each of the children into their respective hiding place to complete the level. Don't forget the statue in this area.

Beaver Dam

Finally, a place of refuge. Mr. Beaver's smart little cottage in the middle of a pond, made available by his dam, is just the place to relax after all the fighting.

Weaken the Ogre

There is only one objective: defeat the Ogre. This is easier said than done and requires that you keep dozens of Ghouls and Dwarf archers at bay, all while attacking the brute. There are five normal statues here, and one that is revealed using the Stone Song.

Keep an eye on the Ogre's health indicator at the top of the screen. When it drops to zero he is defeated.

Bonus Items

There are four bonus items in this chapter. Two are in the barrels at the lower end of the clearing. One is received when you activate the green note in the middle of the clearing. The final bonus comes from defeating 20 Ghouls.

While simultaneously defeating Ghouls, attack the Ogre. Any of the older children are good for this. Keep an eye on everyone's health and use the health powerups and Lucy's healing ability to keep everyone alive.

Bonus Items

Hidden Statue: Have Susan use the red note near the top of the clearing to find the hidden statue.

After the Ogre has absorbed quite a bit of damage (though his indicator won't have dropped much), a picture of Lucy appears near his head. Lucy must attack the Ogre. She climbs on him and begins beating him about the head.

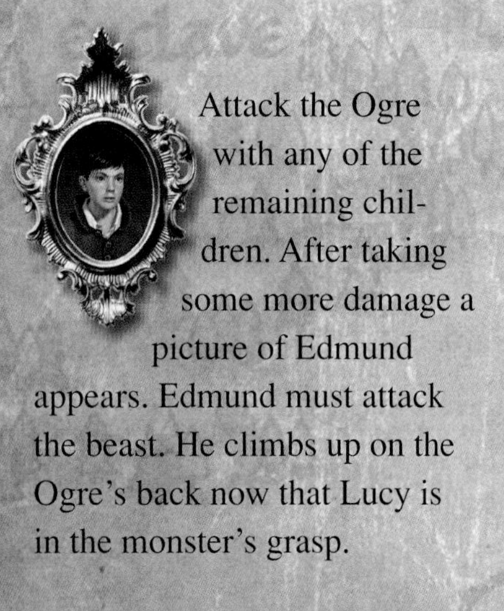

Attack the Ogre with any of the remaining children. After taking some more damage a picture of Edmund appears. Edmund must attack the beast. He climbs up on the Ogre's back now that Lucy is in the monster's grasp.

Only Peter and Susan are left to attack. Continue attacking until Peter's picture appears. Attack using Peter—he clamps the Ogre's club to the ground, making the creature especially vulnerable.

TIP

Sharp Shooting: The small path area at the bottom of the clearing is a good spot for Susan to fire arrows from. There is little room for Ghouls to get in past the hulking Ogre, making Susan less vulnerable.

You now have no choice but to attack with Susan. Her arrows deliver the most damage, so back off from the Ogre and fire arrows as quickly as possible. Eventually the Ogre flings everyone off him and begins to attack again.

Take Out the Archers

It takes three of the team attacks to finally beat the Ogre. Unfortunately archers come to the aid of the brute. Before Lucy or Edmund climb on the monster's back, the archers must be defeated.

Susan's arrows are the only weapons that defeat the archers, who are standing up in Mr. Beaver's pond. Even one archer can stop Lucy or Edmund, so make sure all the archers are gone before moving against the Ogre again.

With the archers out of the way, repeat the Lucy-then-Edmund-then-Peter-then-Susan attack.

When the Ogre throws off the children the second time, more archers arrive—defeat them, then repeat the attack on the Ogre to finally finish it off.

10 Through the Tunnel

After learning of the White Witch, Aslan, and Edmund's treachery, the remaining children must flee Mr. and Mrs. Beaver's house through a tunnel. The Witch's Wolves pursue them.

The Objectives

There are three main objectives in this chapter. First, keep Mr. Beaver safe, so he can chew through the exit. Second, keep the entrance secured. Third, fend off the Boggles trying to make a stone bridge.

Only Susan with her bow, and arrows, and Peter with his Lion's Leap can perform two of these jobs. This chapter requires a lot of running back and forth between the entrance and the Boggle area. If you pay attention to the timers at the top of the screen and force your way through any Ghouls that block your path, you should be fine.

Bonus Items

There are 13 bonus items in this chapter. Two come from the green notes, a third is awarded for defeating 60 Ghouls, and the remaining 10 are given each time you score a 10+ hit chain hit combo (10 enemy hits by Peter without missing or being hit in return). It is easier to do this with the stick, as the sword does more damge making long combos rare.

Immediately after entering the tunnel, Mr. Beaver heads off toward the exit. Along the way, he is taken by a Ghoul—a tough Ghoul. Peter is the best person for taking out this Ghoul, though it requires far more than the normal number of hits to defeat it.

Protect Mr. Beaver

Tip

Leave Mr. Beaver to the Ghouls: Only temporarily, of course! When he is taken hostage, he is not harmed; he just cannot help the children. The first time Mr. Beaver is captured, try not to kill the Ghoul that's taken him until you are ready for him to begin chewing through the exit. No attacks from the Wolves or Boggles take place while Mr. Beaver is captured the first time.

This means that all but one of the bonus items and all but three of the statues can be collected before having to deal with time limits. When you have the nine accessible statues and 12 of the 13 bonus items, rescue Mr. Beaver.

When Mr. Beaver is safe, he heads to the exit and starts to chew through the roots covering it. This can take a while and he will be kidnapped several more times before he can finish his work, so you need to rescue him multiple times.

The other two objectives have time limits, so you may have to temporarily sacrifice Mr. Beaver to ensure that the Boggles and Wolves do not gain entry to the tunnels.

Secure the Entry

Mrs. Beaver is holding a gate closed that keeps the Wolves back. When each group of Wolves arrives, you must send Susan to shoot her arrows through the entrance to defeat them, or use Peter's Lion's Leap to defeat to Wolves quickly.

It takes approximately 45 seconds for the Wolves to break through the gate, so it's very important to get Susan there as quickly as possible each time a new wave of them arrives. Susan is also able to shoot the Wolves from next to the bonfire.

Fend off the Boggles

Across the gorge, two of the Boggles are trying to topple a large stone so the hoard down below can climb to get into the tunnel. To prevent this, Susan must use her bow to defeat the two Boggles. This can get a little difficult as other Boggles are climbing up the stone pillar that reaches into the gorge.

Bonus Items

The last bonus item is located here. It is accessible from the green note in the center of the platform.

Hard to Find Statues

Some statues in this chapter are a little out of the way. Two them are located on the small pillars on either side of the main pillar in the Boggle area. Another is hidden and is only revealed when Susan plays the red note just above the Ghoul area. The final one is just above the red note on a small shelf.

11 Frozen Lake

No sooner do you escape from the cave than the Wolves move out into the open to attack. They are the least of your worries in this chapter; soon you encounter Boggles, Ghouls, rock throwing Werebats, and even a group of Ogres.

Defeat the Wolves

As you enter the area you see two strange rocks. Have Susan use her Pan pipe. A red note appears. This reveals the rocks to be hidden statues—collect them.

Bonus Items

There is a bonus item in this area on the ledge above the cave. It is hidden behind the waterfall. Peter can open the cave, then have Lucy enter the cave and collect the bonus item and statue she finds there.

The Wolves begin to attack immediately. Peter must defend your party. Two blows from his sword takes out any Wolf you encounter. When he has a chance, have him attack the log that is blocking your party's progress. Susan can also take advantage of the blue note in the center of the ice to put the Wolves to sleep. Be sure to collect the statue in the lower right corner of this area.

About halfway through breaking up the log, archers appear out of the knot holes. Have Susan shoot them with her arrows, so Peter can complete the destruction of the log.

Defeat the Ghouls

Tip

Thin Ice: Beware of holes in the ice. Although the children can't fall off the edge of the ice, they can fall into the holes.

Once through the log, Ghouls drop another log stopping you in the next area. The weak part of this log is blocked by an ice wall that can only be broken by having Susan and Lucy use their team up attack on it. Unfortunately, while you are trying to do this, the children are attacked by Werebats, an archer on shore, and a lot of Ghouls. There are three statues in this area. The one on the ledge can only be acquired using Susan's snowballs.

Bonus Items

There is a green note on the ice here, a bonus at the edge of the ice, as well as a barrel containing a bonus item up on shore.

Once the ice is out of the way, have Peter attack the log to break it up. Susan can use the blue note to halt the attackers for a short while.

Defeat the Ogres

The best defense is a good offense, especially in the next part of the lake. Two Ogres stand on the shore throwing large rocks, while Boggles stream in from a cave. Halting these two attacks is your first priority.

Bonus Items

There is a bonus item in one of the barrels at the water's edge. Beware, though, as these barrels blow up when hit. Have Susan attack them with arrows from a safe distance.

The pile of rocks to the left of the Ogres is unstable. Have Susan fire her arrows at it. After a few shots the pile tumbles down and crushes the Ogres.

Just to the right of this pile is another unstable pile. Have Susan shoot this one, too. It blocks the Boggles. Your only threat now is the occasional Ghoul...and the Ogre that fell in the water earlier.

Use the Pan pipe on the blue note in this area to slow down the Ogre. This gives Peter enough time to cut through the next log. This is a tough log to cut through, so Susan has to do two things to ensure that Peter can break it: she must use snowballs to put out fires that an archer keeps lighting on the log, and she must lull the Ogre to sleep several times.

Survive the Ice

Once through the final log things get a bit easier, except now you are on a time limit—the White Witch is in purusit. The good news is that this means the Witch's power is weakening!

There are three sections of ice that the children must survive to make it to shore. Peter is the best to use here, as he can take out the Ghouls that pop up through holes in the ice fastest. Occasionally a dying Ghoul gives up a thirty second time extension—make sure to grab these. After the Ghouls have been defeated, go around collecting the coins and statues you find.

When each of the first two sections of ice is finally cleared of Ghouls, the ice shifts. The way to the next section is available. Have Lucy find the safe paths, then shift back to Peter for the assault against the Ghouls. Make sure you retrieve the three statues in these two areas.

Getting Ashore

The final section of ice is the toughest. In addition to Ghouls, there are archers, Minoboars, and Boggles. Peter is still the best suited to taking out these menaces. Susan is needed to eliminate the archers on the shore. There are two statues here.

Bonus Items

The two final bonus items can be found in this area. One comes from the green note in the middle of the ice, while the other is in a barrel up on shore. Let Peter finish off all the enemies on the ice before sending Susan after these.

When the final enemy has been eliminated, a final piece of proof arrives that the White Witch's magic is fading—Father Christmas drives up in his sled to provide magic presents to Peter, Susan and Lucy!

12 The Great River

Finally off the lake, the children now have to contend with the great river. With the White Witch's endless winter coming to an end, the river's ice is breaking up. The children must escape the Wolves before the river has completely thawed.

The Giant Waterfall

The children are trapped. On three sides are sheer walls they can't hope to climb. On the fourth, the river's ice is already starting to crack, spelling certain doom for anyone who ventures out on it. While trying to find a way out of their predicament, the children are besieged by Wolves.

Bonus Items

There is a green note that Susan can play in this area that yields a bonus item. Also, if Peter can score a 12+ hit chain against the Wolves, each chain (up to five) is rewarded with a bonus. This is only possible on Hard difficulty. These five may also be taken in the spring clearing later in the chapter.

The only hope for escape is to break the sheet of ice holding in the waterfall. The resulting cascade scatters the Wolves and provides an escape route for the children. The first step in this plan is for Lucy to begin cracking through the ice at the waterfall's base.

TIP

Lucy's Retreat: Once Lucy has cracked the ice she only has a short time to get away from the waterfall before she is pushed into the freezing water.

With Lucy's job done, collect the four statues located on both sides of the area. Susan must now shoot arrows at three different spots on the face of the frozen waterfall—all while fighting off Wolf attacks and playing the green note's tune. Use Peter to dispatch the Wolves.

When Susan has finished with the second attack location on the waterfall, a 30 second timer starts. She must attack the final location as quickly as possible, so that Peter has enough time to complete his part of the escape plan.

A small stump is all that keeps the power of the waterfall at bay. Peter must destroy the stump to release the waterfall's torrent and free the children from the Wolves' immediate threat. When he completes this, the waterfall bursts forth. It shatters the ice the children are standing on, sending them careening down the river.

The Great River

You are now in control of Peter's ice raft as it plummets down the river. If the raft gets caught up on rocks, or if Peter takes too much damage from collisions, he gets thrown off. If this happens you start over again.

Bonus Items

There are four bonus items floating in the river's water. Maneuver the ice raft to retrieve them.

During the final portion of the journey, Werebats drop stones out of the sky and Ogres push over rock pillars. Eventually, you make it to the bottom, where Aslan awaits.

The Spring Clearing

There is no rest, however. In the middle of Peter's discussion with Aslan, Lucy and Susan's screams send him running to their aid.

Maugrim, the White Witch's main Wolf is attacking the girls. He must be defeated or none of them escape with their lives.

Bonus Items

There are bonus items hidden in the three shield stands, barrels, and pavilion table. There is also a bonus item (green note) in the Spring Cleaning area, Any remaining 12+ hit chain bonuses that haven't already been claimed can be taken here.

Maugrim attacks relentlessly. He takes little damage from any of the children's attacks and quickly regenerates. The one hope is to get him in a vulnerable position and press the attack.

Maugrim and his army of Wolves attack in waves. First, Maugrim attacks. When he has taken some damage, he retreats to regenerate and lets his army take over. After that wave has been beaten, he returns.

During the fighting, the small cart by the tree suddenly sprouts an attack target. Have Peter destroy the cart to reveal a cave that Lucy can enter...though she can not enter it right away. As soon as her picture appears on the tree, send her over and use the activate button to have her climb into the tree branches above. Here she is safe from attack.

When Susan's picture appears on the tree take her to it and have her climb. When the last Wolf of the next attack wave is defeated, Maugrim takes hold of Susan's dress and tries to drag her back to the ground.

Peter must now defend his sisters. Attack Maugrim. He takes lots of damage now. He also loosens his grip on Susan and shifts his attention to Peter, knocking him to the ground.

With Peter trapped and immobile, Susan must fire as many volleys of arrows into the beast as possible. Maugrim rolls off Peter and scampers away. Repeat the process until Maugrim lies dead at the children's feet.

Rescue Edmund

Ginarrbrik, the White Witch's minion, has little use for the queen's new "pet" and, since she isn't around, he doesn't have any problem killing Edmund. Luckily, Peter saves the day by cutting his younger brother free as Ginarrbrik is about to strike him down.

Escape, however, is not that easy. The two boys have to fight Ginarrbrik. He is an expert knife fighter. They also fight the White Witch's minions: Minotaurs, Minoboars, Ankleslicers, and Cyclopes.

Fighting Ginarrbrik

Direct attacks on Ginarrbrik are of no use. His expertise in knife fighting means that he can parry any thrust either of the boys try.

TIP

Keep Away: The best defense against all of Ginarrbrik's attacks is to stay away from him. With the exception of his knife throws, if you stay away from the Dwarf, you can avoid taking damage.

Ginarrbrik's Attacks

The key to defeating Ginarrbrik is understanding his four attacks. Each is deadly in its own right and knowing how to avoid them can help ensure the boys' survival. The attacks are listed below in the order that Ginarrbrik uses them: charge attack, Beard spin, jump and throw, and finally the knife swipe.

Run and Ram

The run and ram has Ginarrbrik running as fast as he can and ramming into one of the boys. Luckily he is no faster than either of the boys, so unless he starts when one of the boys is in a vulnerable location, you should be okay.

Switching to the other boy is the best way to escape the Dwarf if he has you cornered.

The Beard Spin

Ginarrbrik's most devastating attack is the Beard spin. It does a lot of damage, and also knocks the boys off balance. When they are off balance, they can't defend themselves. The best defense against the Beard spin is to keep your distance.

If, however, one of the boys gets backed into a corner, the fastest way to escape is to switch to the other boy. This causes Ginarrbrik to change his focus—of course now the other boy is in peril, so you need to keep him on the move.

When this attack is over, Ginarrbrik is left dizzy and vulnerable. This is the moment to attack.

Jump and Throw

This is, by far, the easiest of Ginarrbrik's attacks to counter. He climbs into the central tree and flings several knives at the children. The knives are fast.

If you are close to the tree when he climbs it, run a zigzag pattern down to the far end of the clearing. There you can simply run back and forth and be assured of never getting struck. When he runs out of knives, the Dwarf jumps down and begins his other attacks. There are also barricades at the far end of the clearing that can be used for cover, as well as the tree Ginarrbrik climbs.

The Knife Swipe

This is Ginarrbrik's most straight-forward attack. Parrying can help avoid this attack, though distance is even better. If you are caught near him, parry every time you see his knife arm start to move.

Defeating Ginarrbrik

Bonus Items

There are ten bonus items in this two part area. There are multiple objects that can be set on fire using Edmund's stick, and two barrels that can be smashed. All of these actions release bonus items.

As noted above, Ginarrbrik's only moment of weakness comes after he has performed his Beard spin attack. He is now dizzy and unable to defend himself. Peter's blade thrusts are nowhere near strong enough to do the Dwarf much damage at this point, so another strategy is needed.

When the Dwarf finishes up his Beard spin attack, he is dizzy. Now is the time to get close and attack.

Continue attacking, pushing Ginarrbrik back toward the tree. A final attack results in Edmund shoving Ginarrbrik up against the tree and tying him to it. As soon as Edmund begins tying him up, Peter must attack the Dwarf.

Ginarrbrik slices through his bonds before Peter can knock him out. It takes at least three attack sequences like this to finally defeat Ginarrbrik.

Defeat the First Cyclops

No sooner is Ginarrbrik defeated, than a group of the White Witch's fighters break into the clearing. Although you need to defend the boys against all of the enemies, the one that you are most concerned with is the Cyclops.

The Cyclops can be defeated in many different ways. You can damage him with a bundle of sticks, burning or not. Also, Peter and Edmund's super combo can damage the Cyclops.

Since the other enemies continue to pile into the clearing, there's no point to sticking around waiting for them. Instead, have Peter attack the tree on the right side of the clearing. If you're lucky, when it falls it takes some of the Witch's army down with it.

The boys can now continue into the right-hand clearing. Now is a good time to collect the four statues.

TIP

Leave the Tree Alone: During this fighting, a target mark appears on a tree along the right side of the clearing. Do not attack the tree until the Cyclops has been defeated or you allow more enemies in to attack you.

Defeat the Second Cyclops

BONUS ITEMS

Be sure to light any remaining object on fire and collect the bonus item in the barrel.

Once the 10 Minoboars have been defeated, it's time to retreat once again.

This Cyclops is defeated the same way as the first—roll a burning bundle of sticks into it twice.

Three things make it more difficult this time. The area is smaller, making movement harder. The bundles do not regenerate as quickly, so you can not attack again as quickly if you miss. The only fire initially available is back in the first clearing.

Eventually, your attacks find the mark and the second Cyclops is defeated.

Defend the Rock

As soon as the Cyclops is defeated, the boys must retreat to the top of a large rock. Minotaurs and Minoboars climb up onto the rock and attack. It is now a fight to defeat 10 Minoboars before the boys fall.

Defend the Trees

The boys are now forced to climb two trees in a final fallback position. There's nowhere to go from here and there doesn't seem to be any hope of rescue.

This defense is not difficult—it's just a matter of timing. To knock the enemies out of the tree, just look at which side they're attacking from. When they climb the left hand side, use the left (primary) attack button. When they attack on the right, use the right (ability) attack button.

The climbing creatures come in waves, first up one tree, then the other. As soon as one wave has finished, switch to the other boy and repeat the attacks, pushing the vile adversaries down.

When the countdown timer reaches zero, a herd of centaurs comes to your aid and drives off the enemy. Phew! That was close.

14 Follow Aslan

A public meeting of the great leaders, Aslan and the White Witch, results only in the witch demanding Edmund's life in exchange for his treachery. Though the treachery was not against her, the deep magic makes it her right. Aslan, knowing more of the deep magic than the witch could ever possibly imagine, asks to talk with her in private that very night.

Sensing something awful, Susan and Lucy decide to follow the lion...

Leaving their Tent

Bonus Items

There is a bonus item hidden in the furthest barrel of the group of three, behind where the girls enter this chapter.

On leaving the tents, the girls' path is blocked by a cart and the side street is guarded by a centaur. Knocking down the cart brings the guard running. A means of neutralizing the centaur is necessary for the girls to continue on.

Luckily, there is a blue note hidden underneath a barrel near the cart—destroy the barrel, so that the note is available for use. Breaking up the cart requires that the girls team up. To make sure that Susan can reach the note in time, get them both near the note. Susan must use her ability button to highlight the note. Immediately team up with Lucy and send the younger girl crashing into the cart, smashing it to pieces.

As soon as Susan lets go of Lucy, have her step onto the blue note. Activate it, and play the tune. As the last note comes out of her Pan pipe, the centaur guard drifts off to sleep unharmed.

Down the Side Street

Bonus Items

There are four bonus items on the side street. The first is in a pile of shields, just to the right of the faun's tent, across the street from where the girls enter. (Grab this one before sneaking past the tent.) The second is just to the left of the tent in a large clay pot. The third can be found in the cart diagonally across the street from the second, while the fourth is in a clay pot just before the next barricade.

Susan and Lucy must now sneak their way past a faun's tent. The light spilling out of the flap illuminates the whole street, so there's no possibility of sneaking past... or is there. Have Susan shoot a volley of arrows toward the door. After several shots, the flap drops closed and it takes a moment for the faun to open it back up. Take advantage of the delay and scoot past.

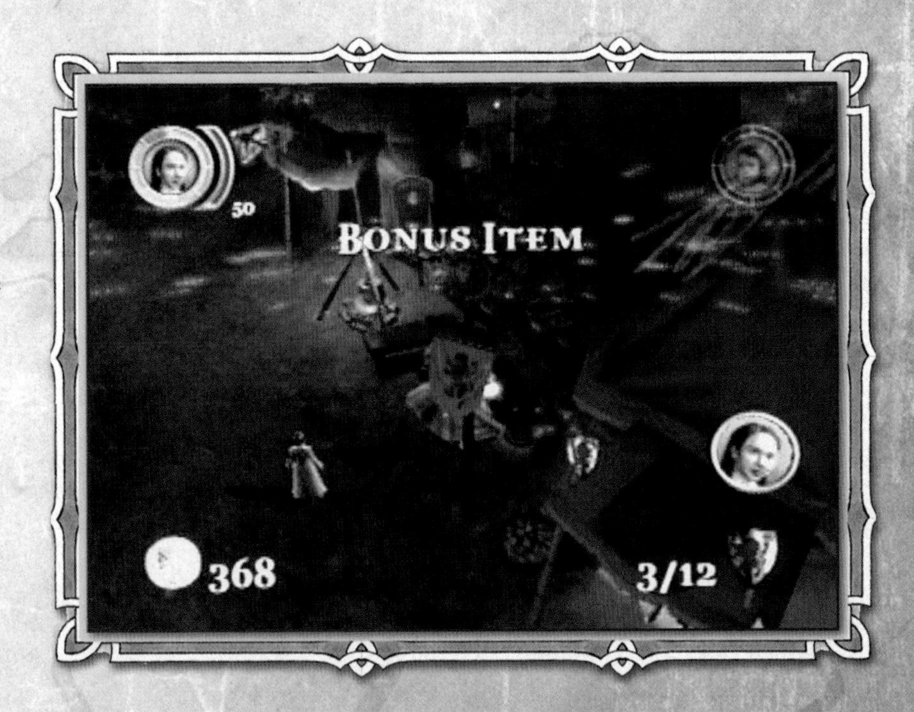

Tip

Don't Get Greedy: There is a single coin right next to the faun's tent flap. Don't go for it or the faun sees you and sends you back to your own tent. This is good advice for all of the tents. It is possible, but difficult, to get the coins outside each tent.

Further along the street is another barricade. You need to break this one down and use the blue note to send the guard to sleep, just as you did at the first one.

The trick here is to wait to break down the barricade until the guard is far enough away to make activating the note and playing its tune easier. You can just make him out as he heads back and forth beyond the barricade. Wait until he is just visible to the right of the right-hand tent, then send Lucy careening toward the barricade. As before, activate the note and begin playing the tune. This time, though, you want to wait on the last note until the centaur is just coming around the corner—this ensures that he is in range of the tune and sleeps.

Onto Main Street

Bonus Items

There are four bonus items a short distance beyond the barricade. All three are in areas where you are safe from detection by the centaur patrols. The first is down the dead end lane to the right. The second and third are to the left of the barricade in the cart and clay pot. The fourth is a green note on the small bypass.

Head up toward the main street, but stop shy of the road itself. Centaur patrols come by this route frequently, so you need to time your next actions well. As soon as the last centaur of a patrol goes by, shoot the flap of the faun's tent directly across the street. This gives you enough time to run into the street, grab a few coins and duck into the bypass to avoid the next patrol.

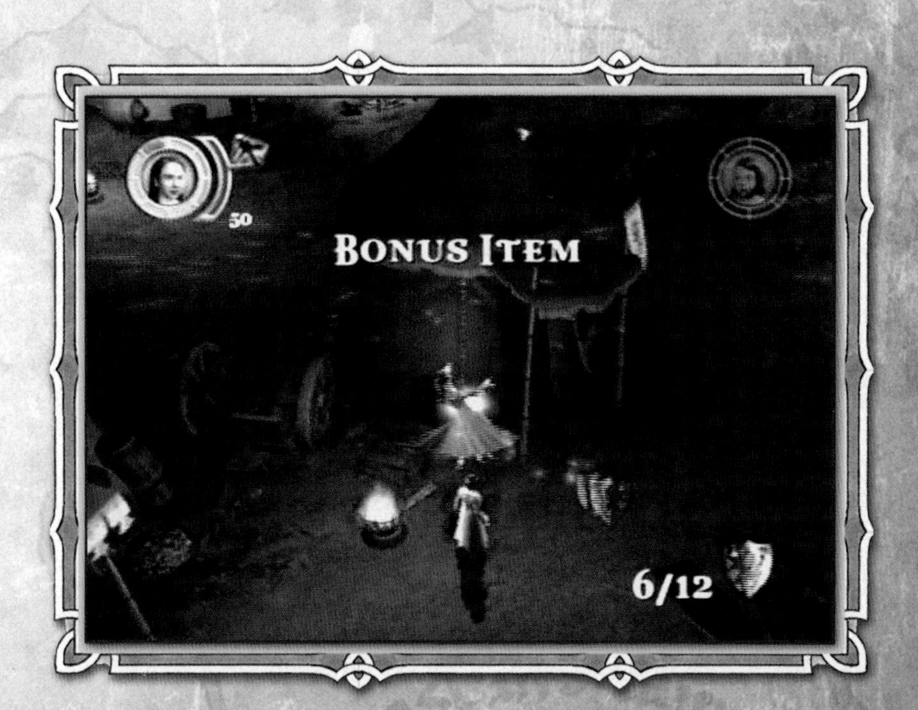

After playing the green note tune, continue along the bypass to the far end. There is another faun's tent across the street. Wait for the next patrol to go by, then drop his flap and head up the street to the right. The centaur patrols now stop, so you are safe from detection.

Bonus Items

There are two bonus items along the main street before you get to the next barricade, both on the left-hand side of the road. The first is in the cart just to the right of the faun's tent, and the second is in the clay pot on the street corner.

The Final Barricade

When you come around the corner you reach the final barricade. This is the most difficult to pass—two centaurs are on guard close to the barricade and a faun is standing at his open tent just beyond.

Although the steps are exactly the same as the previous barricade, this time you have to time it nearly perfectly. Send Lucy flying into the barricade, activate the note, and play the tune all before the centaurs can turn around and move.

Now, before you can go on, immediately shoot out the flap on the faun's tent. The way is now clear...except for the Boggles and Ghouls you see in the distance.

Getting Past the Cyclops

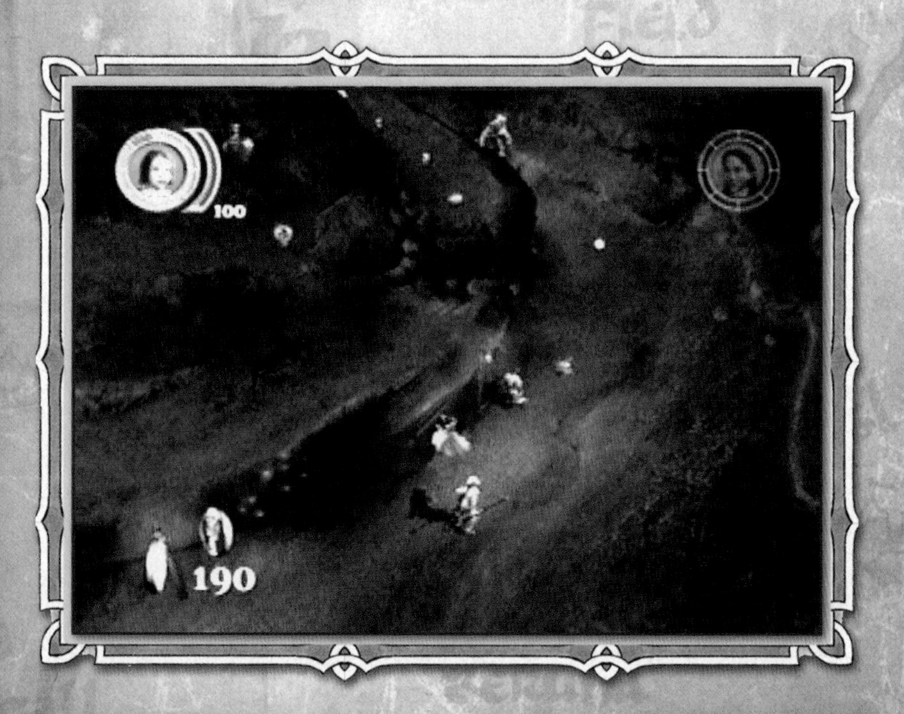

Of course the Boggles and Ghouls aren't the worst things you come up against. Around the corner, is a Cyclops. There's no way you're getting past this guy without a trick up your sleeve. Luckily you've got one. It's just a matter of getting to it.

Up on the ledge, just above the Cyclops, is a blue note. Susan can play it there in safety. Getting to it, however, is a different matter because a rock slide has taken out a portion of the ledge.

There is a cave part way up the path on the left that leads up to a second ledge above the rock slide. Send Lucy into the cave and she pushes more rocks down to fill in the gap.

Susan must get to the blue note. The Ghouls and Boggles come in waves, so try to make it to the note between waves. If you time it correctly you play the tune without being attacked.

The Blocked Path

The girls can now continue on in their quest to follow Aslan. The White Witch's forces have other ideas, though. They've set up brambles across the path and Susan is not strong enough to break through them. Susan can use the fire to make fire arrows. Shoot the burning arrows at the brambles to clear them.

The Witch's forces are strong here, so close to her encampment. The girls have to fight their way past dozens of Werewolves, Ghouls, Boggles, and Minoboars. To ensure victory, target the brambles first. Susan must get close to the fire. Use the activate button to gain fire arrows. You have to fight off enemies, but don't try to defeat them all right now. Collect the two statues at the beginning of the area.

Now run to the first bramble and fire a few arrows into it. As soon as you see the fire begin to take hold, head back toward the bonfire, since the fire arrows don't remain lit for very long.

Repeat this with the other two brambles to clear your way down the path.

Tip

Lucy's Fire-Flower Juice: There are many enemies that need to be defeated. One of the girls will take serious damage, so make sure to keep an eye on their health. Use Lucy's healing abilities to keep them safe.

It's now time to get serious about taking on the beasts that pursue the girls. Susan's arrows are the most powerful weapon available, so use them against the strongest opponents: Werewolves and Minoboars. If you use them against every opponent, then you run out. (Her Gift Bow regenerates arrows over time.)

During this onslaught, the Cyclops wakes up. The time at the top of the screen indicates how much time you have left. There are no time limit extenders in this area. It's vitally important that you take out all of the enemy soldiers. Only when all enemies are defeated are you able to find a hiding place from the Cyclops.

Bonus Items

Bonus Items: There is a green note in the clearing at the far end of the path. If you have time before the Cyclops arrives make sure to get the bonus.

When the last of the Witch's forces is defeated, the tree in the clearing sprouts a target. Collect the three statues around the tree, then have the girls climb up it. From here, you hide from the Cyclops and find out what Aslan and the White Witch have to talk about.

Edmund is safe, but at what cost? Aslan has been killed on the stone table and the White Witch's forces are massing for all out war. Their numbers are far greater than those of the late Aslan's allies.

The small valley of Beruna is to be the site of one of the great standoffs of Narnia's history. Peter and Edmund are to be central to this fight...

Defeat the Giants

Six Giants attack the allies' fortifications. First one Giant attacks, then two. Next, three Giants simultaneously try and overwhelm the defenses. Peter and Edmund are the leaders of the defense—it is their job to repel Giants' support troops. Expert use of the stick bundles can be used to slow the progress of the Giants. But first collect the four statues around the area.

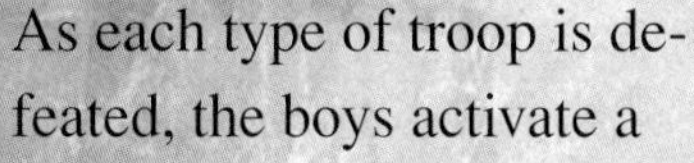

As each type of troop is defeated, the boys activate a trigger that order other defenders to kill one of the Giants either by massed archery attack courtesy of the centaurs, or a hail of large stones dropped by the eagles. Each of the six types of troops (Ghouls, Ankleslicers, Werewolves, Minoboars, Ogres, and Minotaurs, in that order) must be defeated and the trigger tripped before their associated Giant reaches the defenses or all is lost.

Tip

Abilities: Make sure that you check your inventory and have purchased every available combination attack available to the brothers. They need them.

Although you are attacked by enemies, you must defeat the specified number of the specific type of enemy associated with the Giant to enable the trigger.

Bonus Items

There is only one bonus item that you can pick up in this chapter—it is located in one of the barrels near the cliff. The others are obtained by killing the following number of each type of enemy: 30 Ghouls; 30 Ankleslicers; 20 Minoboars; 6 Ogres; and 10 Minotaurs. Don't worry, there are plenty of each.

This chapter is a true test of your combat abilities. Though you have had close combat with the White Witch's minions before, never have you faced so many at one time, and in such unrelenting battle. Narnia is in your hands.

Defeat the Ghouls

When the first Giant climbs over the cliff, you must defeat 10 Ghouls, then track down the trigger that alerts your archers or eagles to fire. Use stick bundles to push the Giants back if they get too close to the archers. As you've seen before, the Ghouls are not terribly difficult to defeat—two power attacks and they're history. Don't waste your ability power on these weak adversaries, as this only drags you down for your upcoming and much more difficult opponents.

Defeat the Ankleslicers

The hardest part about taking out the 15 required Ankleslicers is seeing them! They are so small compared to the other monsters littering the battlefield that you can sometimes miss them.

Luckily, one hit is all it takes to kill the little beasts, so to defeat 15 all you have to do is take 15 strikes! Again, don't waste your combination attacks on these little guys—unless there are a large bunch of them that you can take out with a single high powered attack like lion's leap.

Defeat the Werewolves

The next Giant has a defensive cadre of Werewolves. The one saving grace here is that they do not use their devastating howl attack. This makes them a much more reasonable opponent.

To activate the trigger for this Giant, you need to defeat eight Werewolves. You shouldn't have to worry about using combination attacks against the Werewolves.

Defeat the Minoboars

Minoboars are your toughest opponent so far. The Minoboars are the first opponent to be defeated while trying to best the three Giant team attack. As such, how quickly you defeat them sets the timing for the remaining two opponents. Defeat the Minoboars quickly and you have plenty of time to take the Ogres and Minotaurs. Defeat them slowly, however, and you may never make up the lost time.

If you feel that you're taking too long on the Minoboars, then you should definitely look into using a combination attack such as Minoboar Bane. Once again, use the stick bundles to keep the Giants at bay.

Defeat the Ogres

Ogres are tough nuts to crack. Though you only have three to kill, you should head right into them with the Ogre Bane combination attack—three quick attacks and you can run right to the trigger and activate it. This gives you the maximum amount of time to spend trying to kill the Minotaurs.

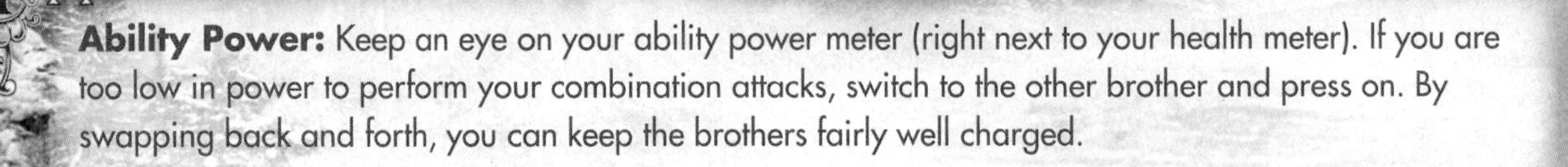

Tip

Ability Power: Keep an eye on your ability power meter (right next to your health meter). If you are too low in power to perform your combination attacks, switch to the other brother and press on. By swapping back and forth, you can keep the brothers fairly well charged.

Defeat the Minotaurs

Other than what is yet to come, the two Minotaurs that you have to defeat now are your most challenging opponents. Don't even waste time with "conventional" attacks. Go right in with lion's leap, which can be used by either brother, and Peter's shield slam.

Although you can beat the Minotaurs with your swords alone, the Giant you are fighting would have long since climbed up over the defensive cliffs and beaten your centaur archers to a pulp.

With the final Minotaur out of the way, you can finally activate the last trigger and have your archers or eagles eliminate the last threat...or is it?

Otmin

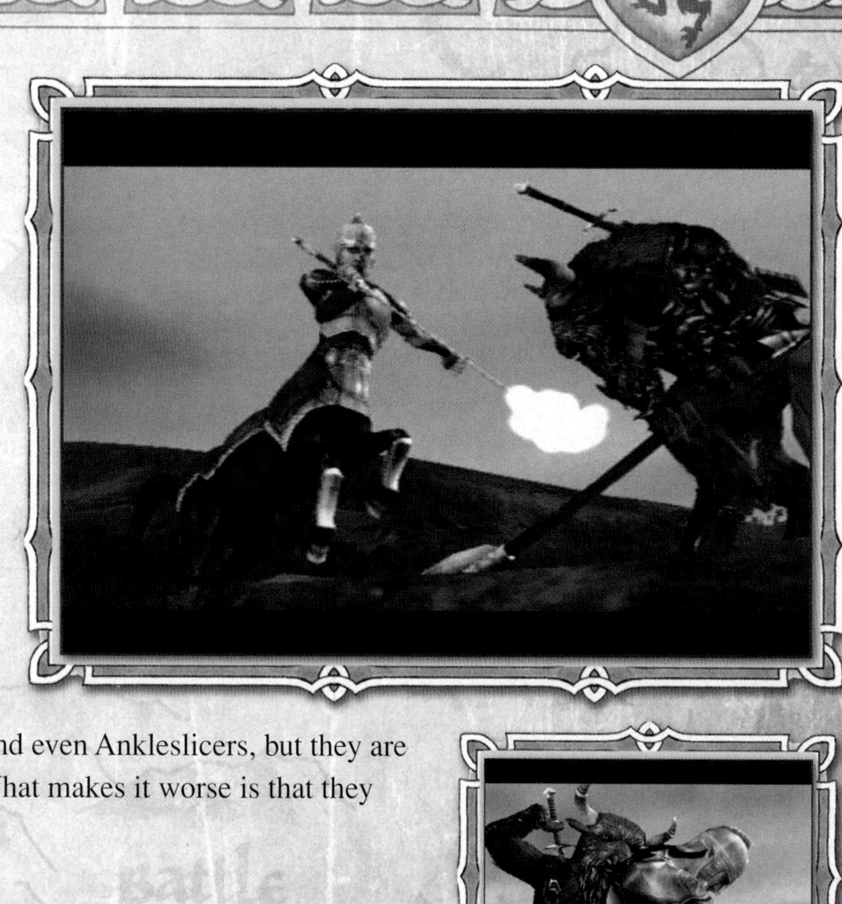

The entire time you have been fighting against the White Witch's minions, Oreius, the centaur captain, has been fighting against Otmin, the Minotaur captain. When the final Giant is vanquished, however, the great beast decides that the boys need to be killed.

This is now a fight that is beyond all you have done before. You are beset by Ogres, Ghouls, Minotaurs, Minoboars, and even Ankleslicers, but they are as nothing compared to Otmin. What makes it worse is that they are all attacking at once!

You take plenty of damage, but dish out even more. Make sure to pick up every heart powerup you can find to ensure that you can keep the battle going.

Otmin must be hit with two stick bundles to destroy his armor. Even then with combination attacks, it takes a while before Otmin begins to show signs of weakening. It takes many, many lion's leaps, shield slams, and lion's roars to harm the Minotaur.

Eventually, when his strength is down by about 30%, you can start connecting with some major plus attacks and these really take their toll.

Finally, a few well placed combination attacks, mainly Peter's shield slam, brings the Minotaur to its knees and Oreius finishes him off.

The victory is bittersweet following on the White Witch's treacherous murder of Aslan...

The Witch's Castle

The Witch has prepared her forces for battle. Her castle has been emptied. The whole courtyard is filled with the stone statues of those who have dared oppose her.

Susan and Lucy must work their way through the castle and help Aslan free the poor souls whose only crime was loving freedom and liberty.

The Courtyard

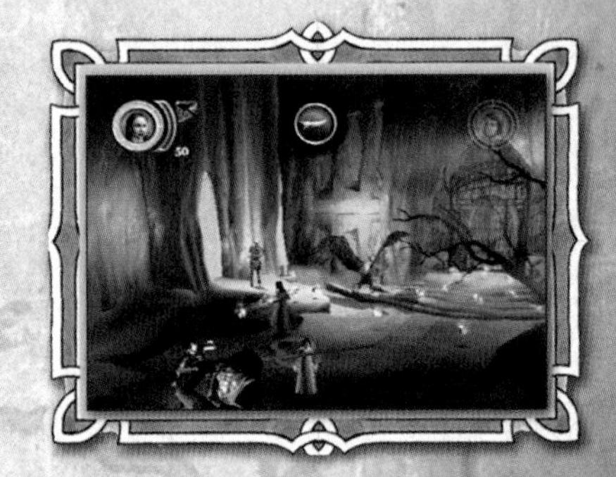

Each section of the castle is blocked by a gate that can only be opened by one of the freed statues. Lucy and Susan must collect all the statues, then gain Aslan's aid in restoring them to health before they can move on.

The first section is the easiest to deal with. There are no enemies to deal with here. You just need to collect the statues by hitting or shooting them.

When all five statues have been collected, a golden note appears on the ground. Have Susan stand on the note, activate it, and play the tune it displays. Aslan comes in and breathes his magic breath upon the statues, bringing them back to life.

One of the restored statues moves to the door and forces it open, allowing the girls to proceed.

The Throne Room

Many of the statues in the throne room are spellbound by Horrors—wispy, elemental creatures of pure evil that the Witch uses to do her bidding. To cast off their dark shadows, Susan must shatter the darkened windows behind each of the enslaved statues.

This forces the Horrors away from the statues, so that either girl can move in and collect them.

The Horrors don't leave the room and the broken windows let in a pack of Wolves. While the Horrors don't do much damage, they can be annoying. The Wolves, on the other hand, can be more than annoying if the girls are not vigilant in defeating them.

Bonus Items

There is a green note in the center of the throne room.

Tip

Wolf Tame: Lucy can use her Wolf tame ability to jump on a Wolf and use its strength against the others in its pack.

Move quickly to collect the statues, so that you get to the antechamber and away from the Wolves. As soon as the last statue has been collected, send Susan to the newly revealed golden note and play its tune.

The Antechamber

Once the door to the antechamber has been opened, head through and collect the two statues located there, then go up the stairs to the small room leading to the audience chamber.

Bonus Items

There is a bonus item hidden in the cold brazier in this room. Have Susan drag it over right next to the one that is on fire. As soon as the burned out brazier catches on fire, the bonus has been gained.

There is a single statue in this room, covered by a Horror. Have Susan shoot out the window behind the statue, freeing it from the Horror, then she can collect it.

With the Horror buzzing about, team up the two girls and fling Lucy toward the ice pile blocking the exit. Move the girls into the audience chamber.

The Audience Chamber

This room is crawling with Horrors and there are no windows to let the sunlight in. The only option is to destroy the room itself.

On each of the two raised viewing stands on the side of the room is a stalagmite with a target on it. Have Lucy enter the caves on each side of the lower region to get to the viewing stand. She can hit the stalagmites causing them to weaken.

It's now Susan's turn to shed some light on the subject. Aim her arrows at the stalactite in the ceiling and fire a couple of shots. The mass of ice comes crashing to the ground, pouring sunlight over the Horrors and rousting them from their perches on the statues.

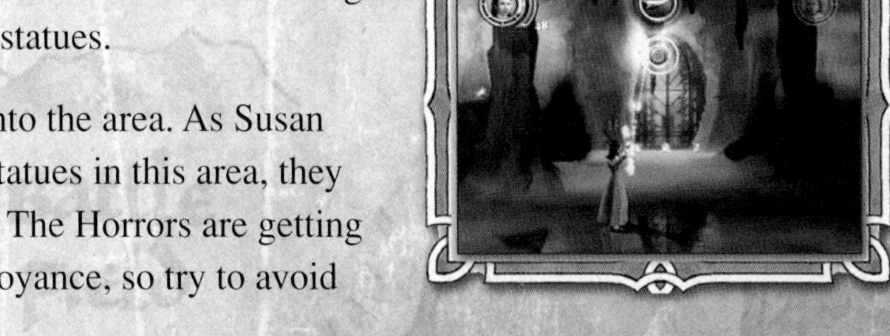

Again, Wolves come swarming into the area. As Susan and Lucy work to collect the four statues in this area, they must also fight off the Wolves and Horrors. The Horrors are getting larger, becoming more of a foe than an annoyance, so try to avoid their touch when possible.

After the four statues have been collected, play the golden note and get out of the audience chamber by going down the stairs at the far end of the room.

TIP

Wolf Tame: Again, Lucy can make short work of the Wolves by employing her Wolf tame ability.

The Holding Room and Dungeon Entrance

At the bottom of the stairs is a small, rather unremarkable room...until the Boggles show up.

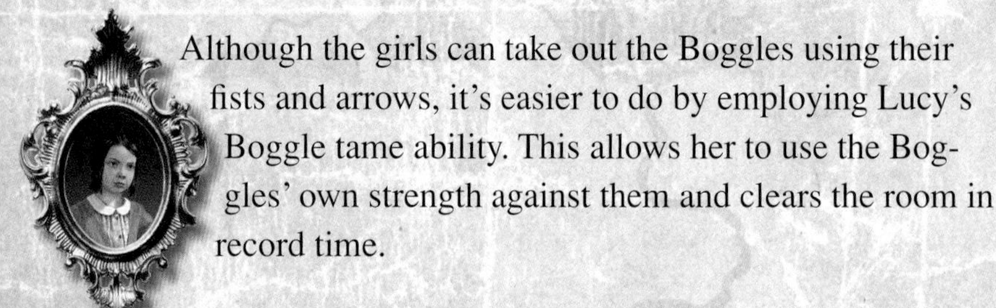

Although the girls can take out the Boggles using their fists and arrows, it's easier to do by employing Lucy's Boggle tame ability. This allows her to use the Boggles' own strength against them and clears the room in record time.

Unfortunately, the Boggles do not know when to quit. Wave after wave of the pale creatures comes pouring into the room. The only way out is past the ice pile opposite the entrance.

TIP

Team Up: The fastest way to access the tame Boggle ability is for Lucy to team up with Susan. When she is flung at a Boggle she hits it and hops right up on its back!

Team the girls up and send Lucy careening into the pile of ice. It shatters, leaving the exit clear.

The exit is clear, but not safe. Heading out onto the ledge reveals that it's terribly thin and, as the Boggles illustrate, not very strong.

When they come climbing back up, have Lucy again use her tame Boggle ability to keep the girls safe. Eventually another section of the wall tumbles down and the girls can continue on their way to the dungeon entrance.

Finish off the few remaining Boggles that follow you and continue into the dungeon. The dungeon entrance is the room immediately after the ledge area.

BONUS ITEMS

There is a green note in the dungeon entrance.

Dungeon

As soon as the girls enter the dungeon the wooden stairway under them collapses—they must either complete this area or perish!

BONUS ITEMS

There is a green note in the center of the dungeon.

Again, this area has no windows to be smashed open letting in light and Horrors. The Horrors have become even more aggressive and dangerous. You must be swift in finishing up this room.

Near the entrance is a fire that Susan can use to make fire arrows. Fire these arrows at each of the Horror-infested statues to drive off the evil smoke and collect the statues. Of course now the vaporous menaces are after the girls!

The exit door is now available. Bring Susan up to the door and have her attack it. No sooner does she land her first blow than...

an Ogre crashes through sending her to the ground. You now have to contend with both Horrors and an Ogre. You can not defeat either of the enemies, so you have to escape. Get Susan to work on the door and bash it in as quickly as possible.

Tip

Evasion: The Ogre is slow. Use this to your advantage by running to the right side of the room to draw out the Ogre. When it gets close, scurry to the door on the left side and bash it in. It may take several times running back and forth, but it can make the difference between opening the door and becoming a welcome mat in front of it.

On the other side of the door a golden note awaits Susan.

Bonus Items

The brazier on top of the golden note holds a bonus item. Unfortunately you need to light the brazier to collect the item and you no longer have access to fire arrows. Since the only source of fire is all the way across the dungeon, you must drag the brazier that whole distance to collect the bonus. Be ready to switch from Susan (who can drag the brazier) to Lucy (who can heal her wounds) as the Ogre and Horrors do not stop their attacks simply because you've opened the door.

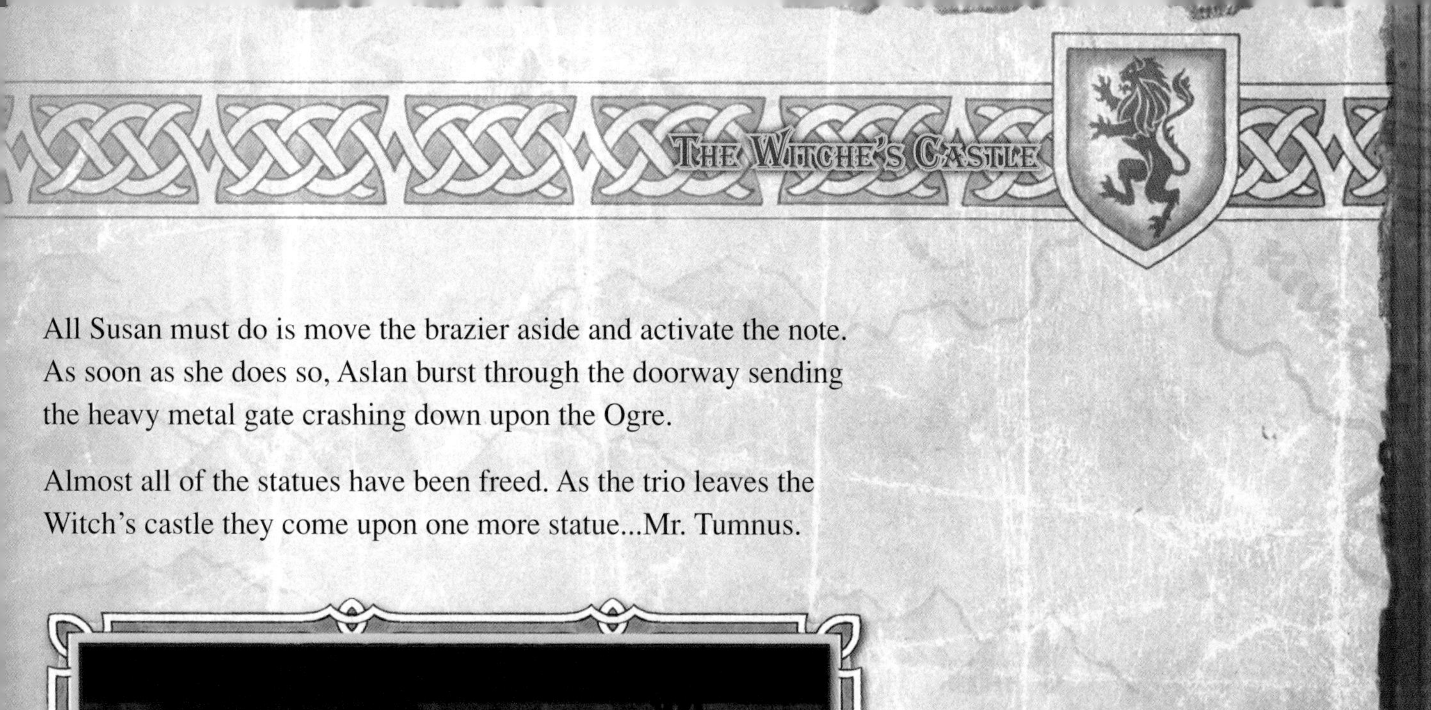

All Susan must do is move the brazier aside and activate the note. As soon as she does so, Aslan burst through the doorway sending the heavy metal gate crashing down upon the Ogre.

Almost all of the statues have been freed. As the trio leaves the Witch's castle they come upon one more statue...Mr. Tumnus.

17 The Great Battle

The White Witch's magic has been banished from Narnia and springtime reigns throughout the land. The evil ruler still remains, however, and her forces have yet to admit their defeat. Great armies of foul beasts march to battle against Aslan's soldiers.

In the middle of the battle, all four Pevensie children must prove their mettle by turning the tide of battle. It is only through their efforts that the White Witch's hold over Narnia can finally be destroyed...

Bonus Items

There are seven bonus items in the level. Six can be acquired by executing 10+ chain hits, while the last is a green note in the middle of the battlefield.

The Scope of Battle

Though the earlier battle of Beruna pitted Peter and Edmund against a large force, the scale of the Great Battle is enormous. There are two things that keep this engagement from being overwhelming: there is no time limit and there are no Giants.

Aside from those differences, the thrust of the battle is essentially the same—you must fight off waves of massed enemy soldiers to ensure that the forces of truth and justice reign supreme.

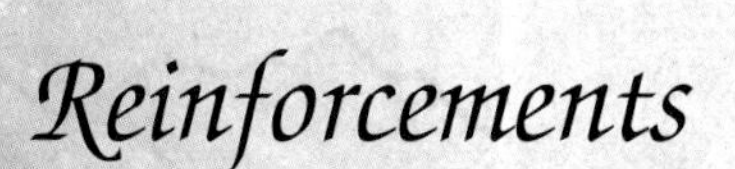

Reinforcements

The statues that you have collected throughout the other chapters finally come in to play. You may now call upon them during the battle as reinforcements.

The number of each type of reinforcement you can recruit is based on the number of statues you collected throughout the previous chapters. The number of statues each type of reinforcement costs is directly related to how effective it is—the more damaging a set of reinforcements, the more statues it takes to recruit.

At the beginning of the mission you need to select the type of reinforcements you would like to recruit. There are four different types, and their effectiveness varies.

- **Phoenix Barrage:** A phoenix rains fire down on your enemies. This is a particularly lethal attack that can make short work of all of the enemies.

- **Arrow Barrage:** A group of hidden archers sends a volley of arrows at your enemies. This is the weakest attack, the arrow barrage is a good way to distract the enemy, but it doesn't do much damage.

Centaur Charge: A herd of centaurs race over the plateau and flatten everything in their path (except the children, of course)—a devastating attack.

Eagle Strike: A flock of eagles drops large stones on your enemies. Any creatures that aren't defeated are knocked back and are easy pickings for the children.

Tip

Wait: Because of the limited number of reinforcement calls you can make, hold off until you absolutely need them. Typically you want to use your reinforcements to get you out of a tough jam—say when a large number of enemy soldiers are massed around the children and you are having difficulty killing them all. In this case, reinforcements can be terribly useful in clearing the battlefield and giving you time to regroup before more creatures attack. Though you can use reinforcements to help complete attack waves, there are usually not enough of a particular race of monster on the plateau at one time for this to be effective.

Note, the number of reinforcements you select is the number of times that you can call on that reinforcement throughout the chapter. For example, if you recruited three eagle strikes, then you can call for an eagle strike three separate times throughout this chapter.

The Attack Waves

In this chapter, there are nine separate waves of attackers that must be defeated. You must kill a specific number of each type of enemy to complete the wave. The monsters get reinforcements. These monsters do not directly advance a wave's progression, failure to defeat these additional troops could result in a main character's death.

The nine waves are made up of the following combinations of creatures:

1. Ghouls
2. Ghouls and Ankleslicers
3. Ghouls, Ankleslicers, and Dwarf Archers
4. Ghouls and Werewolves
5. Minoboars, Werewolves, and Dwarf Archers
6. Minoboars and Minotaurs
7. Minoboars, Minotaurs, and Ankleslicers
8. Minotaurs and Ogres
9. Minotaurs, Ogres, and Minoboars

Each of these waves is indicated by the icons at the top of the screen. The number next to each icon shows how many of the particular enemy you have to defeat to finish up their part of the wave. When you have finished off one race, the icon is grayed out.

Except for the Dwarf Archers, every one of your adversaries climbs onto the plateau to do direct battle with the children. The archers, however, sit nice and cozy across a valley and lob their arrows at the children from a safe distance. Susan is the only one of the Pevensies who can return fire and eliminate the archers.

The Battle

There is no one way to win The Great Battle—or rather there is *every* way to win it. What this means is that *every*thing you have learned about combat throughout all of the previous chapters must be included here.

Peter and Edmund are used the most in this chapter because of their great offensive strength. Susan and Lucy are important for their specific skills: Susan's long range attacks and Lucy's healing ability, respectively.

Combination Attacks

The boys possess some pretty nasty combination attacks. You must use these attacks to their fullest.

Of particular importance are the Bane attacks—Ghoul Bane, Minoboar Bane, and Ogre Bane. Using these attacks, especially when the beast is a specific part of the wave you are fighting, can greatly increase your victory.

Take full advantage of lion's claw, lion's leap, and lion's roar. They are vitally important to putting down each wave quickly.

Team Up Maneuvers

Team up attacks and defenses are also important. By combining the strengths of the children, you enable attacks that are greater than anything the children can do separately.

Of particular use is Peter and Susan's team attack. When you need to take out the Dwarf Archers across the valley, Peter can handle the short range attacks needed to ward off the enemy. This allows Susan to use her arrows to attack the archers when the immediate area is clear.

Victory

As mentioned earlier, victory is achieved by making use of every scrap of offensive and defensive art you have learned up to now.

When the last Ogre, Minotaur, or Minoboar (depending on which creature of this wave is the last to die) finally expires, the children have carried the day.

There is still one opponent to defeat and she is the most deadly of all...

The White Witch

The final showdown is at hand. With most of her forces decimated, it's time to expel evil from the land. The four children must now take on the White Witch herself and bring her despotic reign to an end.

The Sequence of Battle

There are four main parts to this battle:

- **Army Attacks:** The Witch's forces attack the children.
- **Witch Attacks:** The Witch herself attacks alongside her soldiers. Since the Witch is invulnerable to the children's advances, they must avoid her while still battling the army.
- **Children Attack the Witch:** When the Witch is vulnerable, the children attack and weaken her.
- **Aslan is Victorious:** When the Witch is sufficiently weakened, Aslan steps in for the final blow.

When the chapter first begins, the children are immediately setup for fighting the Witch. This is the only time that they do not have to combat her minions before taking on the ruler herself.

Except for "Aslan is Victorious", the other parts of the sequence get repeated as many times as necessary to weaken the Witch. For example, near the end of the battle, each of the fire attacks that weaken the Witch only do one-third of the damage necessary to bring in Aslan to save the day, so you have to do the entire sequence at least three times.

Bonus Items

There are five bonus items available in this chapter. One is a green note that Susan can play on her Pan pipe. The others come from achieving 10+ chain hits.

The Witch's Army

There are two different parts of the battle; fighting the Witch and fighting her army. In the Great Battle, you proved that you are more than a match against her forces. The White Witch has saved her big hitters for the end; she adds Cyclopes and Werebats.

The "Standard" Army

You meet up with all of the monsters you fought against in the Great Battle. Since you have made it this far, you have shown great ability in defeating the Witch's minions.

In this battle, you have to use all the same cunning and ingenuity you did in that last fight. Remember to make good use of your combination and team up attacks.

Cyclopes

During this chapter you have to defeat two Cyclopes to proceed. Although you can defeat them with an extremely large amount of team attacks, or by shooting them with Susan's bow, it is far quicker and less dangerous to hit them with two bundles of burning sticks.

Tip

Fire: The two bundles of sticks that are effective against the Cyclopes are those that are located near the fires.

You have to roll the sticks into the fire and then send the bundle into one of the Cyclopes. Edmund and Peter are the only ones capable of pushing the bundles around. This does half damage to the Cyclops. You have to hit each one twice. All of this, while fighting off Ogres, Werewolves, and all of the other White Witch's creatures.

Werebats

The Werebats drop large stones on the children. The way to avoid being hit is to turn the child you are playing sharply when a Werebats begins to follow him or her.

Battling the White Witch

Absolutely invulnerable to all attacks, the White Witch is the toughest opponent you meet during this entire chronicle. Her only time of weakness comes after she has expended her energy on her ruthless attacks.

The White Witch Attacks

Each time the White Witch enters the battlefield, she lands near her platform at the top of the clearing. She lands with such force that the ground buckles under the strain and all the children are sent crashing to the ground.

She enters the field and begins her attacks. Since she is invulnerable at this point, the only defense is to keep away from her. Make sure that the children run to the far side of the clearing and stay on the run until the Witch has returned to her entry point.

Tip

Monsters: The Witch's army is still on the field of battle, so you have to contend with them as well.

During the later parts of the level, if the Witch gets within striking distance, she casts a spell that incapacitates all the children except Lucy. The youngest Pevensie child needs to use the healing abilities of her fire-flower cordial to awaken the others, so that they can continue the fight.

The White Witch is Vulnerable

After using up her energy, the White Witch retreats to rejuvenate herself. She does this retreat in two steps: first she jumps to her entry spot and rests for a moment before jumping further back, out of range of the children. She is vulnerable to attack only after the first jump—if you wait too long and she retreats fully, then she regains her invulnerability.

Two attack sequences are needed to defeat the White Witch:

1. Used at the beginning of the battle, this sequence involves the three oldest Pevensie children. Peter attacks first, then Susan with her bow, then Edmund.
2. Employed after the first has been successful twice. Susan attacks with her bow, then the Witch must be hit with a flaming bundle of sticks, and finally Peter attacks. This sequence must be completed successfully three times.

Peter's Attacks: Peter must strike the Witch five times in quick succession and get a 5+ chain hit. During the first sequence, Peter is the first to attack and he must do so while the Witch is vulnerable at the top of the clearing. During later sequences, he is the last to attack, and does so after she has been hit by the flaming bundle of sticks.

Susan's Attacks: Susan fires arrows at the Witch. She must shoot the Witch twice in the first attack sequence. She must score five hits on the Witch in the second attack.

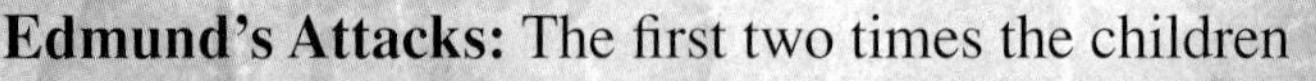

Edmund's Attacks: The first two times the children attack the White Witch, Edmund must attack after Susan. The second time he achieves his 5+ chain hit, he breaks the Witch's wand. She retaliates by stabbing him with it. Though he doesn't die, he is incapacitated for the remainder of the battle.

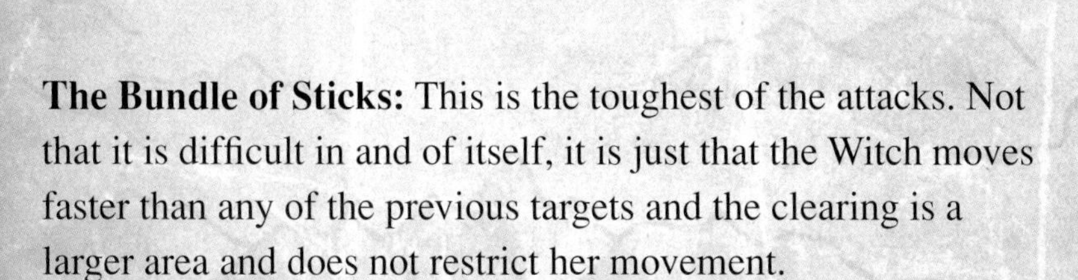

The Bundle of Sticks: This is the toughest of the attacks. Not that it is difficult in and of itself, it is just that the Witch moves faster than any of the previous targets and the clearing is a larger area and does not restrict her movement.

TIP

Hurry: All of the above steps have a fairly short time limit. If, for example, you are not able to hit the Witch quickly enough with the burning bundle of sticks, she returns to her safe haven and the sequence starts over again.

Final Victory

The third time Peter is able to do his 5+ hit chain on the burning queen, a golden note appears on the ground. Susan must play the note to call Aslan to their aid.

The note is played none too soon as the White Witch is about to kill Peter! Aslan saves the day by jumping on the queen and crushing her—much to her surprise since she didn't know he had been resurrected.

Each of the Pevensie children is then installed as a queen or king of Narnia, to preside over the land in peace for years and years to come...

GameBoy Advance

As a special bonus, we've included this walkthrough for the GameBoy Advance version of *The Chronicles of Narnia: The Lion, The Witch, and the Wardrobe*. Be sure to read chapters 1, 2, and 3 to learn about the characters you meet during your adventures.

Lucy Meets Mr. Tumnus

Follow the other children to the wardrobe. When they leave, Lucy must enter it to travel to Narnia!

Move north to meet Mr. Tumnus. Follow him to his cave and help him by moving rocks and clearing piles of snow.

Follow Mr. Tumnus back to the lamppost and kick the creatures that try to stop you.

Follow Mr. Tumnus back to the lamppost. On the way you encounter enemies. Defeat them with a kick. You also solve rock and snow puzzles. Before reaching the lamppost you learn to collect and use items in your inventory.

Edmund and the White Witch

Playing as Edmund, head north to reach the lamppost. Beat up the Dwarfs and other creatures that attack you. You meet the White Witch, who gives you some enchanted Turkish Delight and talks to you about bringing your brother and sisters back to Narnia with you.

After the White Witch leaves, head back to the lamppost to meet Lucy.

Through the Wardrobe

TIP

Multiplayer: You can also play this chapter in multiplayer mode as any of the four children. In single player mode, you play as Lucy.

Edmund broke a window in the library, so now all the children have to hide from Mrs. Macready, the Professor's housekeeper.

Follow the other children into the wardrobe room and hide inside it—suddenly you are all in Narnia!

After everyone apologizes and you take some fur coats from the wardrobe, head off to Mr. Tumnus's. Look out for Dwarfs and other creatures along the way and defeat them as necessary.

When you reach Mr. Tumnus's cave, it has been ransacked by the White Witch's soldiers!

Follow Mr. Beaver and help Mr. Squirrel by finding his missing family heirloom and returning it to him. When you return the heirloom, you are awarded Aslan's Song.

Forest Passage to the Beavers

TIP

Multiplayer: You can also play this chapter in multiplayer mode as any of the four children. In single player mode, you play as Peter.

Go north (up) toward Mr. Beaver's home. You have to fight many Dwarfs, Wolves, and other creatures to reach it safely.

When you reach a log that you can't move, and the forest animals don't respond to the call of Aslan's Song, defeat the Dwarfs and Wolves that are scaring the animals. Then return to the log and try again. Two reindeer come to your aid now.

Continue on your way and, after defeating several more Dwarfs and Wolves, you arrive at Mr. and Mrs. Beaver's house. Here you learn more of Aslan and his plans to end the White Witch's reign in Narnia.

Searching for Edmund

TIP

Multiplayer: You can also play this chapter in multiplayer mode as any of the three remaining children. In single player mode, you play as Peter.

While everyone else was chatting with the Beavers, Edmund has run off to see the White Witch. You must find him before he betrays you all.

Follow Edmunds footprints, watching out for the Minoboars and other enemies. Defeat them to keep yourselves safe.

To get past the ice wall, build a fire at the top of the ramp, use it to light Peter's stick. The stick melts the wall when you attack it. You may have to return to the fire a couple of times to finish melting the wall.

Mrs. Bear asks you to find her son. Track down the cub and lead him back to his mother. She helps you move some large rocks when you call her using Aslan's Song. Continue on your way, clearing out any ice walls with Peter's flaming stick.

The Long, Cold Walk

This chapter follows Edmund's climb up the mountain to the White Witch's castle. Although there are no enemies to defeat, you need to defend against the snowy wind that tries to beat you off the mountain trails.

To climb the mountain, move to one of the rougher parts of the cliff wall and move up to start climbing. Watch out for the winds and move toward the direction the wind is blowing from.

Move quickly to keep from getting too cold and pay attention to the fire that you come across—you may have to backtrack to get to a fire to warm yourself up.

Dash to the Tunnels

You play as Susan. She and Mr. Beaver are setting a trap for the Wolves. Head right and when you reach the bridge, move the rock back to block it—this slows the Wolves.

At the second bridge, you need to destroy the ice pile before moving the rock.

On the plateau, Mr. Beaver asks you to hold off the remaining Wolves while he sets a trap. Use your snowballs and speed to avoid theses Wolves as they cannot be kiled. Mr. Beaver calls to you; run down the ramp, which falls trapping the Wolves.

Escape to the Enclave

TIP

Multiplayer: You can also play this chapter in multiplayer mode as any of the four children. In single player mode, you play as Susan.

Although you are now reunited with Peter and Lucy, you are immediately attacked by Boggles. Defeat them quickly and move on.

To get past the blockade of stones, use Strength of Character to lift one of them out of the way. Continue on your way, going mostly left.

Eventually you get to the Guardian Boggle. The only way to beat him is to hit him three times when he is holding up a boulder to throw at you. When hit, he drops the boulder on his own head. The third boulder defeats him.

Edmund in the Witch's Castle

To escape, move the left-hand rock to expose a tunnel. Enter the hole and move south to a ladder in the wall. Climb the ladder and speak with the reindeer.

The key is in a chest in the cell across from the one you escaped from. To get there, you must move right from the reindeer's cell, then north. You can avoid or kill guards to keep from being sent back to your cell.

TIP

Guards: Although the guards won't hurt you, if they catch you, you return to your cell and have to start all over again. You can keep from getting caught by punching a guard once, then moving away, or by punching the guard until he is defeated.

Return to the reindeer's cell with the key and unlock the door (move to the door then hit A).

The next key is in a chest at the left edge of the main chamber. Get it, then move down and right to the Bear's cell. Release him and go into the other cell located here. Move the rock and head down—at the far end of the tunnel, you find a chest containing the final key. Go into the main chamber, then down and left to the last cell—use the key to release the fox.

Leave the fox's cell and head left to the staircase—unfortunately this takes you to a room full of guards. After you beat them all, you are caught and taken the White Witch's chamber. Though you haven't escaped, you saved a reindeer, a Bear, and fox from her.

Crossing the Frozen Lake

TIP

Multiplayer: You can also play this chapter in multiplayer mode as any of the four children. In single player mode, you play as Peter.

Move west and defeat the creatures attacking the poor fox.

Go west—you need to call some reindeer to move a log.

Eventually you arrive at Mr. Beaver's home. You are safe for the time being.

As you leave his home, you hear sleigh bells—is it the White Witch? No, it's Father Christmas! His presents are wonderful, new weapons to help you in your quest.

Race to the Great River

TIP

Multiplayer: You can also play this chapter in multiplayer mode as any of the children other than Edmund. In single player mode, you play as Peter.

The other children continue their escape from the Witch's Wolves. Leave the entry point and go right, then up. Break up the ice piles, then move the stones to continue.

Move down the ramp, then work your way around the trees, and continue west.

Head up and, after you reach the deer, go down the ramp. Follow the trees around to the deer's home. Defeat the guards and the deer is safe.

Go back up the ramp and use your Leap of Faith ability to jump the gap between the two outcroppings. You have to battle several creatures, then perform a series of Leap of Faith jumps to reach the end of this chapter.

The Big Thaw

Still playing as Peter, the goal in this chapter is to get across the great river before all the ice melts. Although there is no specific time limit to get across the river, you can only stay on each section of ice for a short period of time before it crumbles, dropping you into the icy water.

Trying to stop you along the way are dozens of the White Witch's soldiers. Only defeat them when there is no other way past them. Engaging in fights with the creatures slows you down; making it more likely you'll fall through the ice. The best strategy here is to run, quickly.

Basically, you will be progressing north (up) the entire mission to reach the shore and meet back up with Lucy and Susan. Your route is: Up, then Right, then Up, then Left, Down, Left, Up, Right, Up.

If the Wolves block your way ashore, don't waste time trying to fight them, run west until you can climb back on dry land. Watch Peter defeat the Wolves and continue on your way…

Journey to Aslan's Camp

Tip

Multiplayer: You can also play this chapter in multiplayer mode as any of the children other than Edmund. In single player mode, you play as Susan.

Starting at the shore of the great river, head right. When you reach the first ice statue, turn north, and take out the Ogre and Dwarf using snowballs. Clear away the snow and continuing on. Walk around the stone wall, then move the stones and snow out of the way.

Head down the ramp. Clear away the snow and continue right and up into the clearing. Now turn right again, and head down the ramp. Continue east to the third ramp—here you can head up without having to clear away stones or snow.

Do battle with the vile creatures you find on this side of the river, then walk across the fallen tree and defeat last few monsters. Continue north (up) to reach Aslan's camp.

Peter's First Battle

In this chapter, Peter must reach Susan and Lucy to protect them from Maugrim, the White Witch's chief Wolf.

Once playing as Peter, head south taking out all the White Witch's minions on your way. Don't rush, Maugrim waits to truly threaten Susan and Lucy until you arrive, so you can take your time and go to all the side areas and collect food from the ice, ice statues, and chests.

Maugrim and his lieutenant are as far down as you can go to the right. Fight the lieutenant first, then defeat Maugrim. He is far tougher than a normal Wolf.

Aslan's Training Grounds

Tip

Multiplayer: You can also play this chapter in multiplayer mode as any of the four children. In single player mode, you play as Peter.

This chapter is all about getting comfortable with the new sword and charge attack before the final Battle for Narnia. As you work your way through the area playing Peter, make sure to use the charge attack.

Basically, keep on the move and defeat the White Witch's minions. Head down, then right, and then down again to a couple of ramps. Cross over the river and defeat everything that gets in your way.

Go down as far as you can, then turn left. Head down into the Witch's army camp. You are vastly outnumbered, but keep up the attack and pay special attention to your health. Eat some food from your inventory, if you get weak. You fight a heavily armored Ogre, when you beat it you have completed your training.

Frozen Allies

After a dramatic cut-scene you, as Lucy, find yourself in the courtyard of the White Witch's castle. After Mr. Tumnus is freed, continue around the courtyard and free the others. When this is complete, move inside and work your way through each of the chambers in turn.

When you battle the Giant, maneuver it over one of the cracked areas of the floor, then hit it repeatedly until it stomps its foot. Do this three times in the same spot and it fall into the icy water below.

The Battle for Narnia

TIP

Multiplayer: You play as Peter, then Edmund, then Peter again.

The showdown is finally at hand. You have to do battle against the White Witch and determine the fate of Narnia. Before you can reach her, though, you need to take on many, many of her soldiers.

Head down until you reach a ramp. Head up the ramp, defeating all of the Witch's minions along the way. Continue down the path to the clearing. There are a lot of tough enemies here, so keep an eye on your health level and take food from your inventory as needed.

Eventually, the call will be given out to fall back. This is when you switch to Edmund. You will automatically be placed at the head of the ramp just below the White Witch. Defeat all of the soldiers you find here, then head up the ramp to confront the icy monarch. You can only hit the Witch while she is casting a spell—don't let her complete the spell or she turns you into a statue. After you have connected several times, her wand will shatter…then she stabs you.

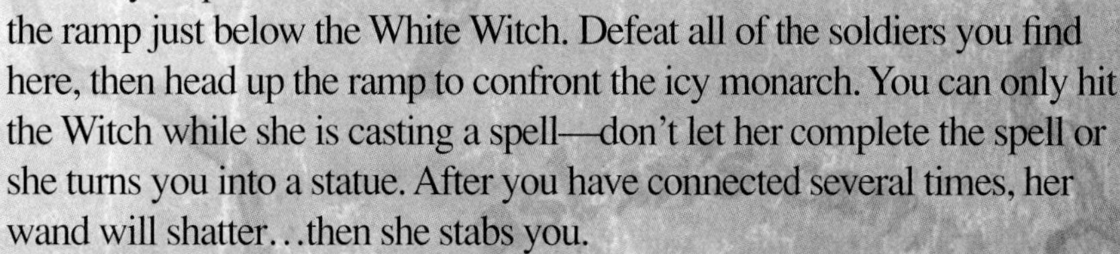

It is now up to the rest of the Pevensie children to defeat the White Witch. As Peter, attack the White Witch. Keep hitting her as fast as you can. Watch out for her spinning attacks, as they deal heavy damage. Eventually she becomes tired and kneels down for a brief time. When this happens, call up the Unified Face nobility from your inventory and attack her again. A single hit with this attack brings Aslan who defeats her.

The Chronicles of Narnia: The Lion, The Witch, and The Wardrobe

After the opening cinematic, you find yourself in control of Lucy. Enter the wardrobe and discover Narnia.

Follow Mr. Tumnus

Walk to the east to meet Mr. Tumnus. After the conversation, follow Mr. Tumnus. You can smash old stumps along the way to find useful goodies, just stand next to one and press the A Button.

Continue east through the Old Path until you reach an ice statue. Hurl a snowball at it by pressing the X Button. You find these ice statues all over. Destroy them to get ice shards. Move north to an ice barrier. Hit the barrier to destroy it and continue up to the Old Clearing.

Mr. Tumnus tells you about the value of ice shards. Grab them along the way. They are needed to purchase various things. Follow Mr. Tumnus north to find the Bear. Don't worry about the thorns, Mr. Tumnus leads you around them.

Let Mr. Tumnus lead the way past more thorns into the Canyon. He clears them so that Lucy can get past. Follow him to the west. Continue following Mr. Tumnus to the north and destroy the ice barrier.

Keep following him past a pond. Watch out for the snow swirls; they hurt Lucy.

Move south. Follow Mr. Tumnus into his house. Talk to him. As you get some much needed rest, he tells you of his adventures.

As Lucy rests, you take control of Mr. Tumnus. After a short conversation with a couple Dwarfs, head west and defeat the rats that come out of the hole. Be sure to grab the ice shards the rats drop.

Continue to the west and take out more rats. The path curves to the north. Follow it until you are blocked by some thorns. Follow another path to the east—defeating any rats along the way. Destroy the lone thorn at the end of the path. This opens up the previous path.

Go back to the newly opened path and continue north. Follow the path to the east to more rats. The path cuts back to the west to the last of the rats. Head back to the east and enter the cave. Examine the gold to start a conversation with a Dwarf.

Follow the Dwarf out of the cave to find the area covered in ice. This ends Mr. Tumnus' story. After Mr. Tumnus apologizes for kidnapping Lucy, he decides to help her get back.

Exit the house and follow Mr. Tumnus. Defeat the Wolf with snowballs.

Follow Mr. Tumnus back the way you came. Keep an eye out for the snow swirls. To the east another Wolf attacks. A couple of snowballs should do the trick.

Mr. Tumnus tells you about the chill factor. The Chill Meter in the top left of the screen shows how cold you are. When Aslan's head turns into a snowflake, you slow down and receive less experience. Seek shelter to warm up.

Follow Mr. Tumnus to a couple of ice barriers. Destroy them and continue along the path. Defeat the Ankleslicers that attack along the way. Attack the lone thorn to open the route.

Follow Mr. Tumnus to meet the Bear in the Old Clearing. He lets you stay at the den to get warm in exchange for cleaning it. Clean the den and rest.

When you exit the cave you find yourself back at Lantern Wastes. After saying goodbye to Mr. Tumnus, exit to the west.

Explore Narnia with Edmund and find Lucy

Now you control Edmund in Narnia. Head to the east and talk to the Dwarf. Walk back to the west and pick up the tree branch. Return to the Dwarf and defeat him with the branch.

Don't forget, you can smash the old stumps with the tree branch to get useful items.

Defeat the two Dwarfs along the Old Path and head north to the Old Clearing to find the Bear. Follow him to his cave. Take care of the Wolves and Dwarfs along the way.

It is here you learn your first talent, Boulder Crush. Exit the cave and follow the small boulders to the west and then north. Some boulders will give you items when smashed, so leave no stone unturned.

Walk north to the Winter Forest and speak to the White Witch. After the conversation, head south and defeat the two Wolves. Continue to the south and west at the next map.

Head southwest and defeat the Dwarfs and Wolves. You can skip this fight, but you miss out on some good experience. If you get cold, seek shelter at the Bear cave.

Continue south, then west along the Old Path. Take out the four Wolves along the way. Move west through the Lantern Wastes area to find Lucy. After a conversation with her, continue west to get back to the wardrobe.

Return to Mr. Tumnus' house

Now you control the whole party. Use L and R to switch control between the children. Enter the wardrobe and head east. Defeat Vardan and his Wolves to lower the thorns.

In the Old Clearing, defeat the enemies and head north. If you are getting cold, use the cave to the east to warm up. In the cave you find the Squirrel Store. You can use the ice shards that you have collected to buy stuff at the store. You can find Squirrel Stores in many caves you come across.

Head to the northwest to find a Horse and talk to him. He gives you quests. After completing the quests, warm up in the cave and head to the northwest into the Canyon area. Wind your way to the north east corner, then to the west to find Mr. Beaver.

Dungeon of Injustice Rescue

Talk to Mr. Beaver to find out that the Queen has arrested Mr. Tumnus. Continue west until you come across another dungeon, the Dungeon of Cowardice. A Squirrel Store is hidden behind the tree in front of the dungeon.

Enter the dungeon and clear out the enemies to the right and the left to get some good experience. Go up the steps in the middle of the dungeon and head north into the next map.

The barriers in this section are random. If one way is blocked, keep exploring until you find a polar Bear. Defeat him and talk to the Dwarf to the north.

This automatically puts you outside the dungeon. Head to the east—making your way to the Dungeon of Injustice. It is marked on the map with two swords.

If you do three quests, you should speak to the creatures again. You might be able to recruit it if your Gentleness is high enough. You can only have one creature at a time.

Make your way around the dungeon in a counter-clockwise direction. Defeat the Dwarfs and rats along the way. You come to a powerful Boggle that guards the Unicorn.

If you are having a hard time with this dungeon, you can go back to the beginning and defeat more enemies to level up. Outside, to the north-east, is a Shelter with a Squirrel Store.

Once the Boggle is defeated, the thorns drop. Talk to the Unicorn and you are automatically taken outside. When you are ready to leave, speak with Mr. Beaver and he takes you to his home. Talk to Mrs. Beaver to find out about Aslan, the King of Narnia. It is here they notice that Edmund is missing.

Find the White Witch's Castle

Now you have control of just Edmund and he wants to see the Queen. You start out at Beaver's River. Follow the frozen river to the northeast.

Defeat the enemies and destroy the statues along the way north. Exit to the Path to the Witch area and continue north to Red Dwarf Peak.

Immediately go to the right. Defeat the two enemies and destroy the statue. Climb the vines on the side of the cliff. Head west and destroy another statue to find more vines. Climb them to reach the next level.

Run straight north and destroy yet another statue to find more vines. Climb them and head north to the White Witch Courtyard.

Head northwest—avoiding the living trees and defeating the Boggles along the way. At the other side of the courtyard you find the White Witch. She locks Edmund up, but not until he reveals where his siblings are staying.

Dungeon of Cruelty Rescue

Now you find yourself back at the Beaver's house in control of the other three siblings. Talk to Mrs. Beaver and she tells you of two dungeons to check out.

Exit the house and walk southeast to Beaver's Glade. Continue to the southeast to find another dungeon, the Dungeon of Cruelty.

Go east then north to get to the top of the room and then head west to find a door to the next map. Enter the door, and make your way west, south, west and north to the northwest corner. There is a boss fight with a Hag. Defeat the Hag and head back east to find the Dryad. Talk to her to free her and you are transported just outside the dungeon.

The Unicorn is to the southwest of the dungeon entrance. Talk to her to do the Unicorn quests.

Move to the west to find the Dwarf Cave. Talk to the Dwarf to get the Dwarf quests. Exit the cave and move southwest. Here you find the Dryad. Talk to her to get the Dryad quests.

Head southwest through the Beaver's Glade and exit west to the Beaver's Forest. Just to the west you find the Satyr. Talk to him to get another quest.

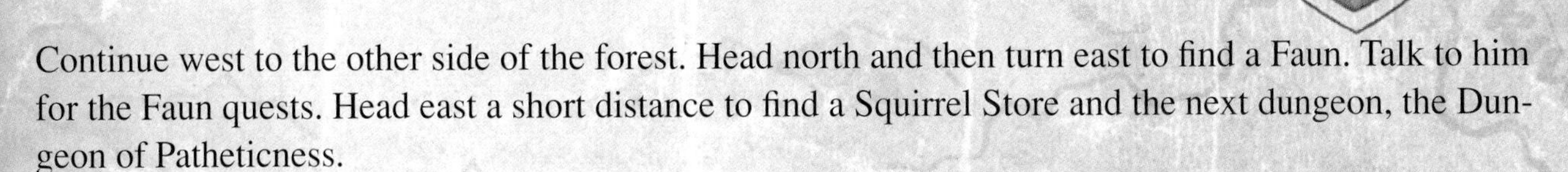

Continue west to the other side of the forest. Head north and then turn east to find a Faun. Talk to him for the Faun quests. Head east a short distance to find a Squirrel Store and the next dungeon, the Dungeon of Patheticness.

Explore this lower section of the dungeon. Watch out for the groups of archers. After you have explored this map, head to the northeast corner and enter the next map. You need to get to a room in the middle of this map. The rock barriers are randomized. Keep searching for the path if you blocked.

In the middle room, defeat the Werewolf to rescue the Satyr. Talk to him and you are transported outside the dungeon.

Find Aslan

You immediately run into the Fox. Talk to him and you are automatically sent back to the Beaver's house. Talk to Mrs. Beaver to find out that the Witch's Wolves are prowling around outside waiting to attack them.

Follow the Beavers to their secret tunnels. Here you find a well and a shrine where you can purchase Blessings, or a Squirrel store. Exit this room back to the tunnels.

Every other route except to the east is blocked by thorns. Go east to enter the Allies Enclave and find Father Christmas. He gives Peter a sword, Susan a bow, and a Lucy a dagger. He also gives you juice that allows Lucy to learn more Cordial Magic. He warns you that the head of the Witch's Police, Maugrim, is nearby.

Just to the north is another Squirrel Store. Move to the east to find Mr. Beaver in front of a well. He tutors you on buying Blessings. Continue to the east to find the Riverside.

Move to the north, defeating the enemies along the way. Talk to the Cheetah to get his quest. Proceed to the southeast and enter the Lake area.

Move directly east to find Naiad. Talk to her to get a quest. Proceed north to the Waterfall and you find Maugrim the Wolf. As you fight him, ice falls from the waterfall. Defeat Maugrim to proceed.

Head back south and then west. Continue to the Allies Enclave to get a quest from the Reindeer. Head back east and immediately go north to find Aslan. Speak with him, then follow him to the north.

Continue to Valley Bridge where you find the Centaur. Speak with him to get another quest. Continue a short distance to the northwest to find the Leopard. Speak to him to get a quest.

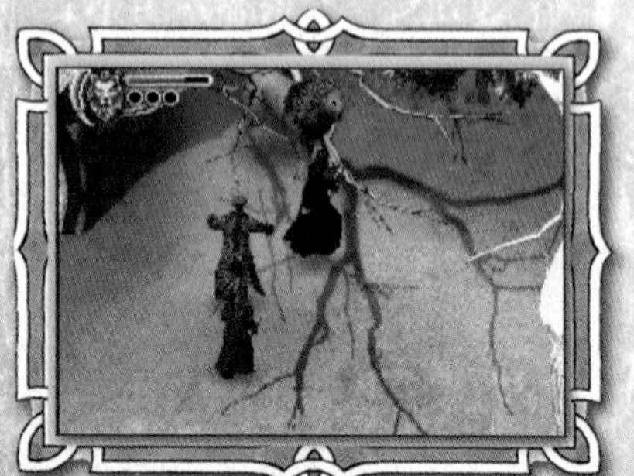

Cross the bridge and head north to find Aslan at his camp. Talk to Aslan. He requests that you find four of his most trusted animal lords that are being held in nearby dungeons. They must be freed before Edmund can be rescued.

Dungeon of Weakness Rescue

Leave the camp to the south and cross the Valley Bridge. Continue south to the Riverside and then head east. Turn north at the Lake and enter the dungeon to the left of the waterfall. This is the Dungeon of Weakness.

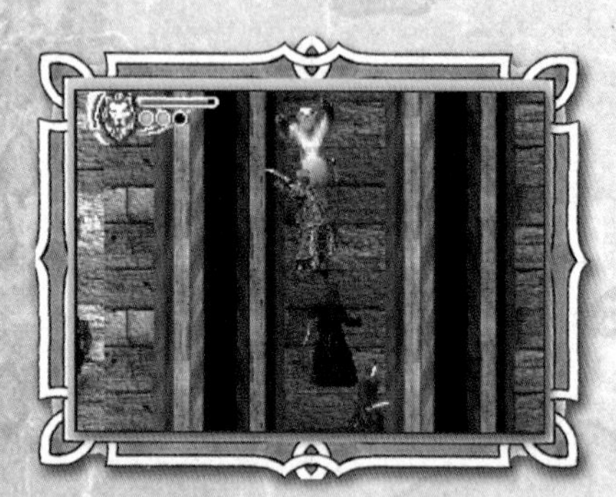

Turn to the east and go up and around to a door in the northeast corner. Enter the door and defeat the enemies inside. Return to the beginning of the dungeon and go west to another door. Enter it and defeat more enemies. This clears the vines that block the center route.

Move up this route to find three doors. Go into the right and left doors first and explore. Defeat the enemies and grab the goodies. After all other areas are explored, go up the center route to a third map.

Make your way to the northwest room. A Minoboar blocks your way. Defeat him and enter the room. Talk to the Gryphon to free him. You are transported outside the dungeon. Move south to the Lake and then go west until you reach the secret tunnels.

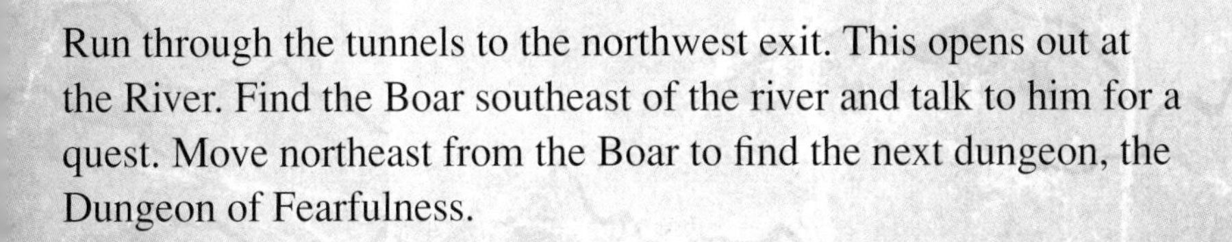

Run through the tunnels to the northwest exit. This opens out at the River. Find the Boar southeast of the river and talk to him for a quest. Move northeast from the Boar to find the next dungeon, the Dungeon of Fearfulness.

Explore the first map—taking care of the enemies and collecting any goodies along the way. Exit through the door in the middle of the north wall. After exploring this second map, enter the center room to the north. Defeat the big Ogre inside to free Naiad. You are instantly transported to just outside the dungeon.

Immediately the Fox tells you that Maugrim is prowling outside Aslan's camp. He is southeast of the camp, near the natural stone bridge. Return to the tunnels and exit to the east to the enclave. Go east and then north to the bridge.

Defeat him to start a conversation with Aslan. He tells you to find another dungeon to the south of the Stone Table.

Find the White Witch's dungeon

Walk south past the bridge, then east past the lake. Move east into the Stone Table Forest. A Squirrel sets up his store for you just inside this forest. Move to the north to find the Eagle. He gives you a quest. Proceed to the northeast corner, into the second map of Stone Table Forest.

On the easternmost side of the map, you find a Squirrel Store. Move to the north then west when you can. After a short distance you find some thorns blocking a path to the south. Hit the lone thorn to get rid of them. Proceed to the west to find the next dungeon, the Dungeon of Severity.

The doors of the two second maps are teleporters. It's possible for you to go in a loop if they pick the wrong door. One door leads to the final map. The other leads to the beginning of the level. Defeat the Minotaur that guards the room and enter. Talk to the Centaur to rescue him.

Return to Aslan's Camp

You are transported outside the dungeon where the Fox is again waiting for you. He says that Aslan needs to see you. Move east, hit the thorn and move north through the opening. Go west to find the Gorilla. Talk to him for a quest.

Northeast of the Gorilla is the freed Gryphon. He teaches the single most time-saving talent in the game, flying you to various locations across Narnia.

Now return to Aslan's camp—past the Lake, Riverside and Valley Bridge. Enter into a conversation with Aslan. Aslan informs you that Edmund is safe and he joins your party. He also tells you that the last lord is located in the White Witch's Camp.

Find the Final Dungeon

Exit the camp and head to the east past the bridge to Valley Forest. The Rhinoceros is standing just inside this area. Speak with him to get a quest. Continue to the east to the White Witch Camps.

Refer to your map and find the last dungeon in the northeast corner of the camp. Enter the Dungeon of Inequity.

This dungeon is one big maze. You must navigate the maze and enter the center room. Make your way to the center—defeating the enemies and collecting the goodies along the way. A Cyclops must be defeated in the order to free the Phoenix. Enter the room and talk to the Phoenix. You are transported outside the dungeon.

The Fox is once again there waiting for you. He has a desperate message that Aslan is about to do something rash. Aslan is at the Allies Enclave near the entrance to the tunnels with the witch.

Return to the Allies' Enclave

Exit the camp to the west and move west to Valley Bridge. Proceed to the south and then west to Allies Enclave. You walk in on a conversation between Aslan and the White Witch.

Aslan tells the children that the Witch no longer wants to harm any of them. Peter and Edmund go to gather an army and you take control of Lucy and Susan.

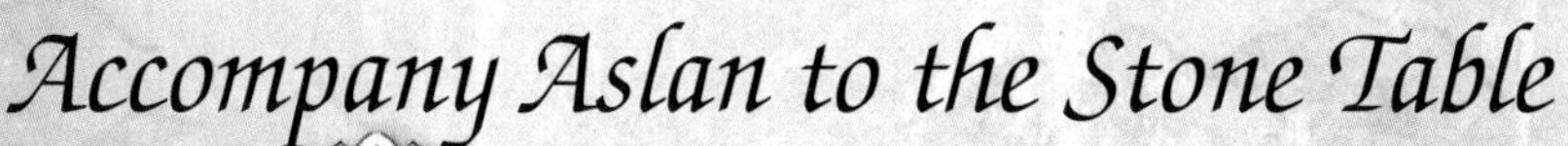

Accompany Aslan to the Stone Table

Return to the Stone Table Forest by running east past the Lake. Cut through the forest to the northeast, then to the east. Move north through the forest to the Stone Table and you witness the White Witch cutting Aslan down.

Walk north to Aslan and talk to him. You are transported to the Waterfall. Walk into the waterfall to enter the Waterfall Cave.

Rescue the Last Prisoners

Walk to the northwest to find a shrine. Just to the east of the shrine, press A by the exclamation mark. This completes the Dwarf quest. Exit the cave and move to the south. The water has thawed, so you must run around the lake and move past the river to the west.

Enter the tunnels and exit to the north to reach the River. Continue north along the Path to the Witch. On the west side of the path, find the Great Dog. Talk to him for his quest.

Proceed north to Red Dwarf Peak. Go east and climb the vines behind the ice statue. Go west and climb the vines behind another statue.

Move north and destroy a third statue to find more vines. Climb them and proceed north to the White Witch Courtyard. Talk to the Centaur; he wants Susan to go ahead through the courtyard. He follows with Lucy.

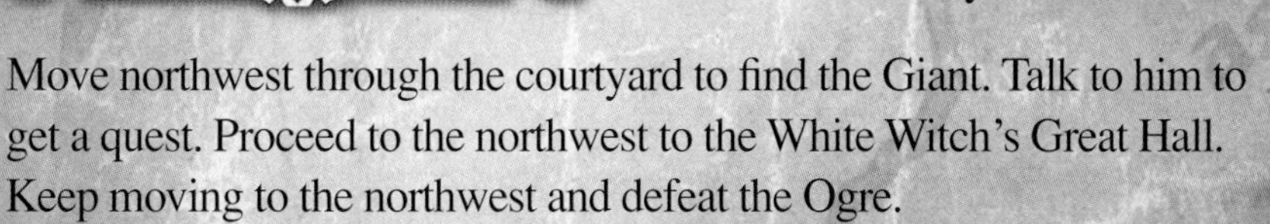

Move northwest through the courtyard to find the Giant. Talk to him to get a quest. Proceed to the northwest to the White Witch's Great Hall. Keep moving to the northwest and defeat the Ogre.

Enter the White Witch Dungeon and Lucy rejoins your party. Walk down the steps to find Ginarrbrik. After a conversation with him, defeat him and walk into the eastern cell. Here you find Mr. Tumnus who has been turned into stone.

Aslan appears and changes Mr. Tumnus back to normal.

Defeat the White Witch

Now you assume control of Peter and Edmund. They are in Aslan's camp. Peter and Edmund must round up the rest of the troops. Take this time to finish up any Creature Quests you haven't done, level up and buy any desired equipment—especially for Edmund.

If you have done three quests, you should speak to the creatures again. you might be able to recruit it if your Gentleness is high enough. You can only have one creature with you at a time.

Once you are ready, speak with the Satyr at Aslan's camp. This takes you to The Battlefield. You must fight your way through the Witch's minions. Thorns appear; they direct you to the correct locations.

You will go east, west and back to the east. Sooner or later you end up in the northeast corner, where Peter and Edmund get separated. Have Edmund talk to the Witch. After a short conversation, you are in a fight with the Witch. Defeat her to win the game.

If you lose to the Witch, you are taken back to Aslan's camp. Either run around and do more quests to level up or talk to the Satyr and try again.

Interview With Douglas Gresham

Please describe your relationship to C.S. Lewis, your personal history with The Chronicles of Narnia, and your role in the creation of the game.

I first read, or had read to me initially, The Chronicles of Narnia when I was about 7 years old and living in upstate New York. Needless to say I was captivated at once, and ever since then at least a part of me has lived in Narnia and a part of Narnia has lived in me. It was only a year or so after that time that I met C.S.Lewis or "Jack" as he preferred to be called, and at the very first I was a touch disappointed. After all I was an eight year old American boy who was meeting the man who actually knew High King Peter of Narnia and the Great Lion Aslan Himself, I expected such a man to be clad in shining armour and carrying a sword, and of course Jack was nothing like that at all . He was instead a middle aged, balding, professorial looking gentleman in shabby clothes. Very soon though the vibrance and vivacity of his personality made up for any visual deficiencies I might have at first regarded him as possessing. We became friends and later we grew closer and closer as Jack became the only stable parental influence on my life. After my mother died, Jack was the one person in the world whom I could lean on and with whom I could share my grief and my troubles. We grew very close indeed in the years between Mother's death and Jack's own untimely demise.

My role in the creation of the games has been one of an advisor on all things Narnian, I have probably been something of a nuisance to the amazingly talented artisans who were charged with the making of the games because of my habit of insisting that things had to be "Narnian". I have also been keen on establishing a game in which success depends heavily on cooperation between players instead of competition, and games that could be played by several players at once. It is very much to the Gamesmen's credit that they have been so successful in translating my wild ideas into some form of reality in the quality games they have built.

What have been the most rewarding aspects of creating a game based on the rich characters and lands of Narnia?

That question almost answers itself. But it's really providing an opportunity for players to actually get inside Narnia and adventure there, and let's face it that's what we all secretly want to do.

What have been most challenging elements of the stories to replicate in an interactive environment?

To start with we have such a wide variety of species and animal characters to deal with, both good and evil. Also trying to bring the magical quality of Narnia to the tiny screens of the games, particularly the hand held platforms.

When did you decide the time was right to expand the World of Narnia from the personal imagination of the reader into the visual and interactive media of film and gaming?

I have dreamed and thought about and planned and schemed this project for more than thirty years I suppose. One of the things that hit two of my children who visited our locations during filming was that suddenly this weird dream of "Daddles'" (that's my family nickname) that they had heard me talking about all their lives was actually real, it was right there happening in front of them. Much to my surprise both Tim and Lucinda were deeply moved by the experience.

One of the most delightful qualities of The Chronicles of Narnia is that they can be appreciated on a simple fantasy level by a child, but are also rich in moral and ethical symbolism with messages that can be deeply moving and profound for adults. How much of this symbolism figures into the game?

I think quite a lot. This is one of the most difficult things to achieve in making a game, I mean the presentation of moral and ethical values. It's a very important aspect of The Chronicles of Narnia that people are able to discover within them, as much or as little symbolism as they seek to find.

I have tried to make sure that this carries forward into the games and thus I think I have probably stretched the Gamesmen to find new levels within both themselves and their art.

Who is your favorite character in the game? Which one do you most closely identify with?

My favourite human character is probably Susan or Lucy, and my favourite non-human is probably Tumnus, but that goes back to the book and has carried forward into all Narnian media. The one I identify most closely with has to be Peter of course. :-)

The children's powers/skills from the books lend themselves perfectly to a multiplayer "party" videogame. Please describe your goals regarding character balancing and battles with Bosses in the game.

I want to make sure that all the characters are equally attractive to play, and to this end they all have to possess certain skills unique to themselves and certain challenges also. They have to be able to react to the differing situations each in her or his own unique way, and that is something very difficult to achieve. We have done this in a large part by attributing to each character a specific skill set and powers complement, and also by crafting the various combinations of the characters that the players have to learn and exercise to achieve specific results.

What did you always keep in the back of your mind when consulting the developers about the creation of the game's characters and environments?

The book, the book, and the book. Everything has to flow from the book to the film and thence to the game. Anyone who plays any of these games should want to see the film and everybody who sees the film should come away from it with a longing to read the book. The game and the movie are gateways along the path that leads to the book, and the book is the real adventure.

I think that once you have read and understood the book and then play the game, the game will seem a lot easier. :-)

If there had been videogames at Professor Kirke's mansion, who do you think would have been the best gamer: Peter, Susan, Edmund, or Lucy? Why?

I find it very difficult to assess that question without my mind automatically referencing the four wonderful actors who played the roles for us. But I really think that Edmund would probably be the best gamer, and in real life I suspect that Skandar (who played him in the movie) probably is too.

Can we expect to see more of The Chronicles made into videogames where players can explore other times and areas of Narnia as the likes of Shasta, Eustace, and Jill?

I really hope so. One of the things that has come out of the making of these games is that we have come up with some wonderful ideas for the future, but we need the hardware manufacturers to leap ahead with the hardware development so that we can incorporate some of our new ideas into the new games without overloading the systems. In any case its been a great deal of fun working with the gamesmen on this project and I would love to do a series each game better than the last and each game pushing the envelope of what is possible to its very edges.

What do you think your step father would think if he could see/play in his Narnia on a videogame console?

Jack would find it an impossibly frustrating experience because he had no top joint in his thumbs, his thumbs would not bend, so he would not be physically capable of playing the game at all! Even trying to would drive him bats. :-D

DISNEY AND WALDEN MEDIA PRESENT

THE CHRONICLES OF NARNIA: THE LION, THE WITCH AND THE WARDROBE

BradyGAMES® Publishing

An Imprint of Pearson Education
800 East 96th Street, Third Floor
Indianapolis, Indiana 46240

ISBN: 0-7440-0619-8

Library of Congress Catalog No.: 2005935363

Printing Code: The rightmost double-digit number is the year of the book's printing; the rightmost single-digit number is the number of the book's printing. For example, 05-1 shows that the first printing of the book occurred in 2005.

09 08 07 05 4 3 2 1

Manufactured in the United States of America.

Acknowledgements

BradyGAMES would like to thank Paul Bodenseik for writing so much so quickly. Congratulations goes out to Dan for a great design and Cheryl for putting up with my ever-constant changes, inserts, and allaround pestering. This book owes everything to Angela Adams. Your extraordinary effort is the reason this book is on the shelves. Take a bow, you deserve it.

BradyGAMES Staff

Publisher
David Waybright

Editor-In-Chief
H. Leigh Davis

Director of Marketing
Steve Escalante

Creative Director
Robin Lasek

Licensing Manager
Mike Degler

Credits

Development Editor
Brian Shotton

Screenshot Editor
Michael Owen

Book Designer
Dan Caparo

Production Designer
Cheryl Berry